SPRINGBOARDS
ideas for drama

SPRINGBOARDS
ideas for drama

JOAN MILLER

Nelson

First published in Australia 1977
Reprinted 1978, 1980, 1981, 1982, 1984

Thomas Nelson Australia
480 La Trobe Street Melbourne Victoria 3000
and in Sydney, Brisbane
and Adelaide.

Associate companies in London, Toronto
and California.

National Library of Australia
Cataloguing in Publication data:

Miller, Joan
  Ideas for drama

  (Springboards series)
  ISBN 0 17 005201 X

  1. College and school drama. I. Title

Printed in Singapore by Richard Clay (S.E. Asia) Pte Ltd.

CONTENTS

ACKNOWLEDGEMENTS

I would like to sincerely and warmly thank all the people who helped to develop my ideas so that this book could happen.

The Principal and Vice-Principals of Malvern Primary School No. 1604 who gave me such a free hand, and the teachers and children who were such a constant and charming source of enjoyment and challenge.

The Principal and teachers of Victoria Park Primary School No. 2957 and the children, with whom I mercilessly experimented.

The Principal and teachers of Burnley Primary School No. 2853 and the children who challenged me to keep things relevant to their needs and interests.

The Principals, staff and children at the following Melbourne schools: Abbotsford, Albert Park, Ashburton, Carlton North, Chadstone Park, Elwood, Flemington, Glen Iris, Kensington, Kew, Port Melbourne, Prahran, Richmond West, St Kilda Park.

The teachers and children whom I met in country centres all over Victoria, who were always so warm, welcoming and enthusiastic.

And my husband Stephen Miller, who not only encouraged me to keep going, but took the photographs to prove that I did.

INTRODUCTION

Dear Teachers,

What you are now holding in your hand is a pure 'ideas' book. It contains hundreds of language activity ideas for children. They can mainly be identified as 'Drama' and 'Spoken Language', but sometimes the activities are unmistakably Mathematics, or Science or Art or Physical Education or Music. All of them, however, have one thing in common; they all involve the children in thinking and planning and testing out and talking and sharing and working with others within a natural social framework. They call upon the skills that children have, in order to solve challenges and problems. On the language side, this seems to happen most consistently in situations when the total involvement method of Drama is used.

I can say this with so much confidence because I have been working with children and Drama for many years — as a classroom teacher with my own grade for five years, then on in-service education throughout Victoria for five years, and now back as a classroom teacher. During this time, I have worked with literally hundreds of children and teachers, developing ideas on the spot, helping teachers plan Drama and Spoken Language programmes, providing activities for all age groups at Primary and junior Post Primary levels. Really, this book is a response to the common question that I have been asked by teachers for so long: 'Where do I get ideas?'

In this book, you will find ideas which will get you started, which will hopefully act as a springboard for your own ideas. Yours will probably be more relevant to your own grade as you will know your children's needs and interests, but sometimes it helps to be given a place to start, and this is what you will find here. Please adapt my ideas freely. **Talk** to your children and **listen** to what they say. **Ask** them what they think, and **include** their suggestions.

As you flick through this book now, you will notice
1 That it is divided into topics or 'themes'.
2 Within each theme the headings are consistent.
3 Individual activities are numbered.
4 There are many questions in each separate activity.
I have done this deliberately, so let's examine each point in turn.

Themes
Many teachers and children are used to working 'thematically'. They find it is more involving and relevant when ideas are linked together by a common interest topic.

INTRODUCTION

Themes give the children a peg to hang an idea on. The children can predict to a certain extent what is going to happen, and this seems to give them confidence and security. I noticed this particularly when working with migrant children who had restricted English. Also, this ability of the children to predict what might happen cuts down on teacher talk, and lets them get on with it. Let me give you a real example that happened while we were taking the photos.

A Prep grade were working on activity 17 in 'The Sea' theme. I asked them to find a partner and work out A and B. This took some time!

Me — 'All the people who are A, crouch down on the floor near your partner. Make yourselves small and smooth and soft. You are a lovely smooth heap of sand on the beach.'

One B child — 'I'm going to make a sand castle.'

Several others — 'So am I.'

Me — (general question to all the B's) 'How are you going to shape the sand?'

All the B's immediately started patting and smoothing and stretching their partners into different shapes. The class teacher and I wandered around asking 'What are you making?' and found that many different animals were being sculpted, some towers with drawbridges and moats, fish, an octopus, a car, an aeroplane.

I was just about to suggest some decorations on the castles, when one child said 'I could use some shells to make my tiger's eyes and teeth', and then she walked around the room searching for shells on the 'sand'. When she had a handful, she proceeded to put them into place on her tiger partner, while she described to me the shape and colour of her shells, why she was placing them in certain positions, and the fact that they made her tiger look 'scary'.

Me — 'Yes, he does look fierce and frightening.'

She immediately latched onto the word 'fierce', and asked another child near her to 'look at my fierce tiger'.

What is going on here, is a group of children being prompted to use their imaginations in such a way that they create things for themselves within the classroom situation. This gives the teacher opportunities for building on and enriching the language that the child already has. Through this type of activity, we are tapping the imagination via suggestions of what to do, and questions which will extend and enrich the doing. We are in effect, creating an atmosphere where things can start to happen.

This is one of the great advantages of this type of informal language work. It frees the teacher to move around and talk and share with the children what is happening. With practice, you develop the ability to be in the right spot at the right time; to pick up what is said by the children and feed it back to them, not so much as an echo, but as a focus point. Perhaps you ask a question that will lead them to further exploration and refinement of their ideas. It is a time when you, the teacher, can find out how the children are thinking and developing problem-solving techniques. And of course, given this information, there is a lot you can do.

Consistent headings

You will notice that each theme is set out the same way: Listening Activities; Looking Activities; Touching Activities; Tasting and Smelling Activities; Exploring Movement and Sound — Individual, Partner and Group; Talking Activities — Partner and Group.

It is done this way because:

(a) All the major areas of Drama are then covered in each theme.

(b) It is easier to locate different sections in the book.

(c) Some sort of working pattern is provided if you need it. You could either work through all the activities in each section as you come to them, or you could make up a session by combining activities from different sections. For example, a Looking Activity, a Listening Activity, three Exploring Movement and Sound Activities, and one Talking Activity would take up about half an hour. Add or subtract, combine or adapt as the mood takes you, depending on the time you have, and the interest span of your children.

Also, the order in which the themes are presented is designed to help. At the start of the school year, 'The Sea' is a favourite topic. 'Machines' next, as the children will be able to draw on a lot of personal experience and observation of all types of machines, and it gives a broad basis for sound and rhythm work. By the time you get this far, both you and the children will be familiar with this style of approach, and be ready to tackle more 'imaginative' themes like 'Witches and Ghosts' and 'Flight'.

Numbered activities

(a) For your own reference, so you can keep track of what you have covered. It is quite likely that you won't always take the activities in numerical order.

(b) To assist you if you haven't done any of this sort of work before. In this case, I suggest you pick out an activity and try it as a five minute break between maths and reading for example,

INTRODUCTION

or in the few spare minutes before lunch time or at the end of the school day. By doing this, if you run into trouble, you can bail out without loss of face as you will be literally 'saved by the bell'. Don't give up though! Think about where it went wrong, and try again tomorrow with a different activity. One of the strange truths about this sort of work is that the children who react in the most frenzied way when they first have Drama experience are the ones who need it the most. Keep trying with them. I have proved dozens of times that it does work.

(c) If you are more experienced or like to have longer sessions, the numbered activities flow together quite well to make a 'mini unit' on one aspect of the topic. In 'Pioneering Days', activities 42 43, 44, 45 and 46 are all dealing with gold discovery, although from different points of view. Also, if you are mixing the activities as suggested previously, the numbers will help you keep track of what you have covered.

Questions within each activity

These are designed to prompt the children to think themselves more deeply into the situation. Some questions are to make the situation more personal, e.g. in 'Pioneering Days' activity 12, there is a question 'What is your horse's name?' If you give him a name he must be your horse. Naming him helps him to exist.

Some questions are to do with relationships between people; e.g. in many of the activities there are 'How do you feel about . . .?' questions. Other questions call out other responses, as you will discover as you go along.

Don't waste your time seeking right answers, because the whole notion of 'right' and 'wrong' answers just doesn't apply. One question can have thirty-five different answers, all of which are acceptable. Look instead for answers that show understanding of possibilities, diversity of thought and development of problem-solving techniques, because it is through these that you begin to understand how the children are thinking, and whether their thinking is helping them solve the problem.

Having now explained what I am 'on about' in this book, let me pass on to you some 'Handy Hints' which experience has taught me in organising this type of work.

1 Establish and use a 'control signal' right from the start, such as a tambourine, cymbal, hand drum, gesture or sound.
   - It is an efficient and pleasant way of getting the children's attention.
   - It helps your sanity, as you can stop all noise when you want to.

2   Have all the children working simultaneously. Drama is doing, not watching others do. This applies whether it is Individual, Partner or Group work.
    - It is easier to handle the children when they are all involved in something, than when half of them are standing around.
    - It removes the audience aspect which can be embarrassing.
    - The shy child gains confidence because he is not being watched.
    - It discourages the 'show off' because he has got no one to play up to.
    - It helps keep the pace moving.

3   If working this way for the first time, pick a spot where you all feel most secure and comfortable. This will probably be your classroom.
    - You and the children will have enough to cope with the first few times, without also being in unfamiliar surroundings.
    - Other teachers and Principals expect a certain amount of noise in classrooms. True?
    - You can launch straight into a Drama activity when the opportunity arises. Concentration and enthusiasm are lost in the trek to the hall or general purpose room.
    - Too big a space is inhibiting for the children. You lose the feeling of 'groupness'.

4   Develop the habit of wandering around amongst the children while they are working.
    - You will find out much more about what is going on, as you will be able to chat to the children, listen to what they are saying, feed in ideas or vocabulary, provide them with feedback when appropriate.
    - You will be able to keep an eye on the known troublemakers.
    - It is more friendly.

5   Give some sound accompaniment for movement — percussion or voice.
    - It is hard to move in complete silence.
    - If you talk about what is happening while the children are moving it will help those who are short of ideas. Example: 'Some people are rocking with their whole bodies. Some are swaying and bending. Some are curling and twisting and stretching different parts.'
    - If the children can make their own vocal sounds while they are moving, it seems to help them with the flow and rhythm.

INTRODUCTION

6 Vary vigorous noisy activities with slower quieter ones.
   - Children get physically tired.
   - We all get tired of prolonged noise.
   - It gives experience in contrasting moods of movement and speech.

7 Don't demonstrate yourself or use a child to demonstrate (except sometimes with non English speakers).
   - Demonstrations give the impression that there is a 'right' way to do it. This is false.
   - Everyone will start to copy each other. Not good for self expression.
   - It slows everything down. You lose pace and concentration.

8 After setting the scene for an activity, give the children time to talk about it before you go on.
   - They'll do this anyway, and you just waste your energy trying to stop them.
   - It is exciting, and the natural reaction is to talk.
   - We want to encourage language, not to inhibit it.
   - You might hear something that gives you a good lead.

9 Pick out the activities you propose to cover before you start the session.
   - You will feel more secure because you have a plan.
   - It will keep things moving. Pace is important.
   - You will get a logically connected flow of activities.
   - It is a record for you of what you did.

Well, that's about all I can tell you. Now it's up to you and the children to see what you can make of these activities.

Do have a go, because you will find that it is worth the effort. Good luck and have fun!

Joan Miller.

THE SEA

THE SEA

LISTENING ACTIVITIES

1 Children relax on the floor and close their eyes.
Listen to the sounds outside the room. Try to work out what is making those sounds.
Pick one sound. You are lying on the warm sand on a beach. Decide what is happening on the beach as you hear the sound.
Tell someone near you what is happening.

2 Children close their eyes.
Teacher makes a sound, e.g. scraping on a table. This is part of the sound track of an adventure film about the sea.
Teacher repeats the sound, then the children open their eyes and quietly tell someone near them what was happening in their film.

3 Children find a partner and decide who will be A and who will be B.
Teacher gives the location, e.g. at the beach, on an island, at a wharf.
A closes eyes. B makes a sound. A keeps his eyes closed, and tells B how he is picturing the sound, e.g. location — a wharf; A thumps the floor: B suggests that a crate is being unloaded on to the wharf.

4 Using a tape recorder
Take a cassette recorder to the sea. Tape the sounds of —
- feet walking in the sand
- feet running in the sand
- feet splashing in the shallow water
- someone diving into the sea

- a group of people splashing each other and jumping around in the water
- the surf
- any sea birds

If you tape the sounds in order, that is, arriving, walking, swimming etc., you will have made a 'sound story' about the sea.

5 How about making a 'sound story' about a trip to the docks? The sort of sounds that could be effective might be —
- travelling to the docks
- walking along the pier
- cranes unloading cargo
- waterside workers on the job
- ships' sirens or other sorts of sirens
- the voices of people

6 Using a tape recorder in the classroom
Try making sea sounds using what is in the room, e.g. crackling paper and cellophane; rubbing floor, blackboard, lockers; drumming on steel cabinets; splashing hands in bucket of water.
Experiment with other sounds and then tape them. Have some trial runs. Talk about them, play them back, find out how effective they were, suggest improvements, find some more sounds. The children will have loads of ideas. Try for different 'moods' of the sea — calm, stormy, rough.

7 Using a tape recorder
Divide the class into six groups.

Each group will be responsible for a sound that shows a different aspect of the sea, or a sound that is heard at the sea. An example of the groups could be —

Group 1 Sound of water
Group 2 Sea birds, such as gulls
Group 3 A family at the beach
Group 4 Someone's transistor radio
Group 5 Lifeguards warning swimmers
Group 6 Power-boats off shore

Tape these one at a time to check how effective they are. Some groups may need to modify their sounds.

Tape the sounds, starting with one group, e.g. the sound of water, and add another, e.g. sea birds. Keep adding the sounds, so that layers of sound effects are built up. The end result will be a general seaside noise.

There could be different endings —
• a gradual fade out
• a lifeguard yells 'Shark!'
• a thunderstorm breaks

LOOKING ACTIVITIES

8 Look at your own hands. Can you make them into the shapes of the different things you can find in the sea?
Suggested topics could be seaweed, coral, different sorts of sponges, starfish, sea anemone, sea urchin, sea slug, turtle, fish, shellfish.

9 Look around the room. Can you see anything that reminds you of the sea? Are there rocks, shells or sand in the room?
Colours of furniture, walls and people's clothing might make you think of the sea.
Are there any colours which are like —
• a stormy sea
• a calm sea on a sunny day
• the feathers of different sea birds
• coral and tropical fish
Talk to someone about what you are thinking.

10 Children find a partner and decide who will be A and who will be B.
A and B face each other. A performs some movement which is related to the sea, e.g. casting a fishing line, swimming, sailing. B mirrors all of A's movements.

11 **With a partner**
Children decided A and B.
You are two seals playing 'follow my leader' in the water.
A is the leader who twists and rolls, dives and surfaces.
B follows all of A's movements.

3

THE SEA

12 You are swimming with your friend, but you are so far apart that you cannot hear each other.
Make up some signals to —
- Get your friend to come nearer.
- Warn him of a big wave about to break behind him.
- Tell him that you are cold, and are getting out of the water.
- Warn him that you have just seen a shark's fin above the waves.
- Ask him if he is hungry.
- Tell him that you have just cut your foot on a broken bottle.

TOUCHING ACTIVITIES

13 Children close their eyes.
You are a tiny sea creature which cannot see, so you capture your food by touch only.
You search around the sea floor, feeling for anything you might like to eat.
Do you find anything? If so, what do you do? You are hungry, so you keep searching.

14 You are wading through knee-deep water at the beach. It is an ocean beach, so the water is tingling cold and clear, with crunching sand underfoot. Every now and then a wave breaks.
What happens to the water level?
What happens to you?

15 It is the end of a hot day at a bayside beach.
Your beach-ball has just floated away, so you have to fetch it.
The water is warm and thick with bits of floating food and newspapers. There is an oily scum on the surface, and drink cans and bottles on the bottom. Sludge squelches through your toes. Ugh!

16 When you open your can of soft drink at the beach, it is too fizzy and sprays all over you. You are sticky and wet all over, even in your hair!
How does it feel?
Does any sand get stuck to you? Perhaps you had better have a clean up in the water.

17 Children find a partner, and decide A and B.
A huddles on the floor. B treats him as a mound of sand, smoothing, patting and making him into

TASTING AND SMELLING ACTIVITIES

a sand sculpture in the shape of a sea creature, coral, a swimmer, a yachtsman, a fisherman, etc.

18 Partners have a group of objects which come from the sea, e.g. rocks, shells, seaweed, starfish, sand. They take turns to close their eyes, and try to identify an object by touch only.

19 You have been playing and swimming at the beach all morning and now you are really starving. The kiosk has all sorts of different food for sale, both hot and cold.
As you wait to be served, the smell of all the hot food, pies and pasties, hot dogs, fish and chips and doughnuts, makes you even hungrier.
What are you going to buy?
How does your lunch taste?

20 You are the sole survivor of a shipwreck and have just made it to a desert island. You were not able to salvage any food from the ship, so you need to discover which plants are edible.
There are some strange looking fruits and berries on nearby trees and bushes.
Do they grow in clumps or singly?
What colour and shape are they?
How do they smell?
Be careful as you taste them!

21 Children find a partner and decide A and B. A and B are sunburnt, tired and happy after a long day at the beach. They have bought some sizzling hot fish and chips from the shop, and are going to eat them out of the paper.
Is there salt and vinegar on the fish and chips?
How do they taste?

22 A has invited B to dinner at his house, and has gone to a lot of trouble to prepare an elaborate seafood meal. It looks and smells wonderful. As B starts to eat —

THE SEA

- A wants to know if B likes the taste of everything.
- B questions A about the method of cooking a particular part of the meal.
- B is enjoying the oysters until he comes to one that tastes just awful. It must be a bad one! What does B do? Does he tell A and risk upsetting him, or does he try to get rid of it quietly?
- A has specially prepared a dish of prawns. B hates the taste of prawns. How can he avoid eating them without offending A?

23 A and B are sharing some strange food.
How do these taste?
- Chips in strawberry jelly
- Sardine ice-cream
- Oyster pavlova
- Seaweed pancakes
- Fish with chocolate sauce
- Penguin pie

EXPLORING MOVEMENT AND SOUND
(INDIVIDUAL ACTIVITIES)

24 You are a surfboard rider waxing your board on the beach.
Is it a brand new board, or have you had it for a while?
What colour is the board?
How big is it? You use a big lump of wax and rub it on hard all over the surface.
Why do you do this?
It is really hard work, so every now and then you rest and check the feel of the board.

25 You are a surfboard rider paddling out to the big breakers.
You might try lying on your stomach on the board, and paddling with both hands. If you get tired of this, you could try paddling other ways.
Small waves wash across your board as you go.
Keep your mouth shut, or you'll swallow water.
Now you are in deep water, and ready to catch a wave.
Are you facing the right way?
How do you sit on your board as you wait?
Here comes a big one. It looks good. Ride it in.
(Provide percussion sounds for the wave, and keep this going as they ride it in to shore.)

26 You are paddling on your surfboard in the deep water. You have been surfing for hours and you are feeling really tired.
Make this the last wave for today. You start to hear a roaring sound behind you which is getting louder. Your board is being sucked backwards! What's going on???

As you glance over your shoulder, you see a huge wave forming behind you. It's a dumper!
What can you do? (Try percussion sounds to build up intensity.)

27 You are going for a swim in the sea to cool off, as you are so hot.
As you wade in, you find the water is really icy. It creeps up to your knees and then to your waist. Brrr.
Perhaps if you wet your hands and rub them on your body, it will help you get used to the cold.
Well come on. You can't stand around like this all day. Plunge in.
How is it?

28 You are making a sand castle on the beach. The sand is damp, and sticks together well.
Do you have a bucket and spade, or just your hands?
Is your sand castle going to be a special shape? Is it going to have holes in it? Will you dig a moat?
This is the best sand castle you have ever made. You might be able to find some shells and seaweed to decorate it.

29 You are a deep sea diver in search of a sunken treasure ship. Your diving equipment is very heavy, and you have to move slowly and carefully along the sea floor.
The only sound is the hissing of the air line coming into your helmet.

How does this sound?
Is the sea floor smooth sand, or scattered with rocks and holes?
Be careful not to lose your balance.
As you move, frightened fish scatter through the water around you. Then in the distance, you can just make out what looks like a sunken ship.
Is this the treasure ship you are searching for? What do you do?

30 You are going scuba diving. You have all your gear heaped in the boat around you, your wet suit, flippers, face mask and air tank.
Do you have a spear gun?
Which piece of equipment do you put on first? You should check that your air tank works properly before you enter the water. How can you test this?
When you are suited up, you sit on the edge of the boat. Are you sure you have everything?
Practise breathing through your air hose.
Now you are ready to drop in. Off you go.

31 You are fishing from a rock that is constantly washed by waves. What sort of fish are you after?
Is the rock smooth and safe, or slippery with slimy sea weed?
Do you have special rock fisherman's shoes to help you keep your balance?
The water boils and surges around your rock, and the tide is starting to come in. Keep watching the tide. You don't want to get stranded.

32 It is a great day for surf fishing.

THE SEA

You have a huge surf rod which you bait up and cast as far as you can. What sort of bait are you using? You are trying to cast out past that line of breakers.

The waves are pounding in, and you have to struggle to keep your balance. Your big rubber waders cover you up to your waist, so you can wade in a bit if you need to.

Are you catching anything?

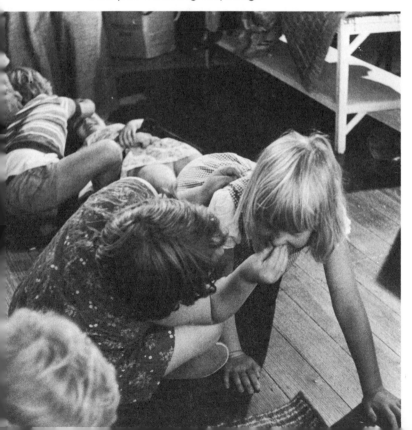

EXPLORING MOVEMENT AND SOUND
(PARTNER ACTIVITIES)

33 You and your friend are collecting shells at the beach. It was high tide this morning, and dozens of pretty, differently shaped shells are marking out the high tide line.

Pick up some shells and examine them. They all have different shapes. Show your friend what you are finding.

What colours are the shells? Do they have patterns and lines on them? You might collect some really unusual ones.

Show each other what you are finding.

34 You are both exploring rock pools. The tide is out so the pools are all uncovered on the rocks. There are dozens of them. Some rock pools are as small as your fist, but a few are as big as the room. They all have interesting things growing and floating inside them.

What can you see?

Here is a tiny rock pool, with little red sea anemones clinging to its sides.

What do they feel like? Try wading through some of the big rock pools. Can you find anything interesting and unusual in your pool?

Talk to your friend about it.

35 You are both playing in the sea.

Is it the ocean with crashing waves, or a bayside beach with still water?

What do you like to do in the water? Perhaps you play a splashing game.

Can you hold your friend's hands and sit on the bottom?

Perhaps you can open your eyes underwater and stare at each other.

Sometimes it is fun to dive through your partner's legs.

You are both having great fun.

36 You are floating in a calm sea on an air mattress that is big enough for both of you to lie on. The sun is really hot, so sometimes you dangle your hands in the cool water, and flick a few salty drops on to your hot bodies. It is very peaceful.

Perhaps you should see how far you have drifted from the shore.

Oh help! You are so far out that you can hardly see the beach!

How are you going to get back?

37 You are professional scuba divers in the clear warm water of the Great Barrier Reef. Your job is to find and remove the Crown of Thorns starfish that is destroying the reef.

These starfish are wanted by a group of scientists who need to study them, so they want them alive and unharmed.

Where are you finding the starfish?

How do you get them off the coral?

How big are they?

The starfish are very prickly, so be careful not to get hurt.

Where do you put the starfish as you collect them?

Every now and then you check your partner to see how many he has collected.

Don't wander too far from your friend.

38 Two smugglers are stealthily unloading contraband from a rowing boat on to the beach.

What is it? How is it packed — in boxes or bags, barrels or bottles?

Is is heavy?

What do you plan to do with it?

It is a dark night, and you don't dare to use even a torch for light in case you are seen. You try to unload quickly and quietly.

Keep a look out for the customs men.

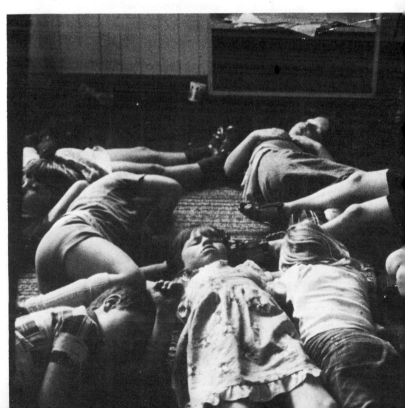

THE SEA

EXPLORING MOVEMENT AND SOUND
(GROUP ACTIVITIES)
Groups of six to eight

Percussion sounds seem to help free children's movements. A tambourine, hand drum or cymbal used to give definite rhythm, or just for background noise, will give the children something to work with.

39 A school of tropical fish is drifting through the water.

It is warm and calm and peaceful. Different sorts of coral grow from the reef, and waving sea weed sways gently around them.

What colours are the fish?

They are all quite small fish, so they like to swim close together. They are timid of dark shapes, and change direction often as they swim.

40 A wave forming far out at sea, building up, then breaking to smash against rocks, or hiss on the sand.

(Slow drumming on tambour or hand drum as the wave builds up. Increase pace and intensity as the wave breaks.)

41 A flock of sea birds fishing far out to sea.

Are there different types of birds?

How calm is the water?

Is it clear or murky?

Are the birds circling in the air, or are some sitting on the water?

What does a bird do when it spies a fish?

What happens if the fish is too big to swallow?

42 Deep-sea creatures searching for food. Where do they find their food? In the sand on the bottom? In ledges, under rocks, among seaweed?

How do they capture and eat it?

Do they move slowly or quickly?

43 Lifesavers rescuing a drowning swimmer.

Do they have all the necessary equipment for the rescue?

Why is the swimmer in trouble? Is he caught in a strong cross current that is rapidly carrying him out to sea? Is he just exhausted and too weak to swim for shore?

Has he been attacked by a shark?

How far out is the swimmer?

Is the sea calm or choppy?

How experienced are the lifesavers?

Who is going to do each task in the rescue?

44 Wharf labourers unloading a cargo ship.

What sort of cargo does the ship carry?

How is it stored?

Is the cargo heavy?

What machinery or equipment is there to help in the unloading?

The foreman would have to check the items as they are unloaded.

45 The crew of a large yacht are taking part in an ocean race.

Where is the yacht racing to?

What season is it?

What are the different tasks that the crew have to do?

Everyone has to work quickly, and as a team.
During the race the weather starts to worsen, as a storm is blowing up. How does the crew cope with this?
What happens to the yacht?

46 A group of native islanders are fishing with nets from the shore.
How do they work together to cast the net?
It is hard work hauling it in.
Did they snare many fish?
What types of fish have they got?
Some fish have torn a gaping hole in the net. How will the natives mend this hole?

TALKING ACTIVITIES
(PARTNER)

47 Children find a partner, and decide A and B.
A is a deep-sea explorer.
B is an intelligent deep sea creature who wants to communicate with A.
Can they work out some sort of common language?

48 A is a deep-sea diver who has recently discovered a sunken treasure ship.
Where did he find the ship?
What does it look like?
What was the treasure — gold, jewels, intricate carved figures?
B is a television compere for a popular national TV show.
What is the show?
The compere interviews the diver about his discovery.
(The compere could take a few minutes to prepare his questions.)

49 A is a fisherman who has just returned to shore after a long hard battle with an incredible sea monster. The monster finally escaped.
B is another fisherman who wants to know what happened.
A might describe the creature's appearance, how he hooked it, what happened during the battle, and how it escaped. B could ask questions about all this.
Does A exaggerate a bit, to make the story more exciting?
Does B really believe all the details?

THE SEA

50 The boss of the pirate gang is dying. He calls his son to him, to tell him where the pirate treasure is hidden.

What is the pirate boss dying of? Is it old age, or some injury he got in a fight?

Is he able to speak clearly, or does he mumble some words?

Do the other pirates know what is going on?

Will this affect the way the pirate chief speaks to his son?

51 Two pirates on a desert island are trying to decide the best place to hide the treasure chest which they have just brought ashore.

How big and heavy is the chest?

What is the treasure inside it?

Does it really belong to these pirates, or have they stolen it from another gang?

Are there some good hiding places on the island already, such as caves behind a waterfall, deep pits, clumps of thorny trees?

Do the two pirates trust each other?

Do they find it hard to agree on the best hiding place?

(This activity could lead into making pirate treasure maps.)

52 Two people are fishing from the pier when their lines get tangled together.

As they are trying to untangle them, both lines start to jerk violently.

They've caught a fish!

But whose fish is it?

TALKING ACTIVITIES
(GROUP)
53 Groups of four or five

A group of surfies are discussing the way they live. All year, they move along the coast, surfing at different beaches.

How do they travel to the different places?

Where do they sleep, in their vans, or in sleeping bags on the sand?

Where do they get the money to pay for petrol and food?

Perhaps some of the surfies are new at this way of life, and the more experienced ones will be able to give them some good tips.

How are they treated by people in the towns, the police and local authorities? What do they like best about this way of life?

What do they like least?

54 Groups of three or four

Some children have just found an old rusty tin trunk washed up on the beach.

It is so rusted up, that the lid is hard to open.

Is there a rusty old padlock?

Perhaps you could smash it off with a rock.

You struggle really hard with the lid. It needs all of you to pull together. Suddenly, it gives way. Inside is . . .??

(Wander around amongst the groups and ask them what is in their trunk. They should be able to describe their find to you. After you have asked most of the groups, sit the children down, and repeat back to them all what you were told by the different groups. This could lead on to some writing or art activities.)

55 Groups of four or six

Some sea creatures have strange names which are partly names of land animals or things, e.g. **dog** fish, sea **horse, star**fish.

Can you think of any others? (Let the children discuss this in their groups.)

What about making up some funny combination names like mouse fish, or sea frog?

In your groups, work out some names. You might like to write them down, describe them to each other, and perhaps even draw them.

(Of course they could use other art media.)

56 Groups of five or six

It is time for lifeboat drill on the luxury passenger liner.

A group of passengers are on the deck near their lifeboat, and a ship's officer is explaining what they should do in case of emergency.

What does he have to tell them?

Does he demonstrate how to put on a life jacket?

Does he explain the way in which they should get into the life boat?

Do all the passengers understand or do some need to ask questions?

One passenger doesn't speak English. How can the officer make sure that this passenger knows what to do?

57 Groups of four or five

Two sailors have just returned home from a long and dangerous sea voyage to Antarctica.

They are telling their families about the adventures they had.

What sort of things do the families want to know?

What was the weather like on the trip?

What happened when the food ran short?

What dangers did they face on the voyage?

The sailors might want to tell about the day they harpooned the great whale.

Will they want to talk about the collision with the iceberg, or is that too frightening to ever speak about?

58 Groups of five or six

Yesterday the lone sailor arrived in port after completing his round-the-world solo voyage.

Today he is holding a press conference for newspaper and magazine journalists.

Which papers and magazines are here, e.g. **Womens Weekly, Bulletin, Sunday Telegraph**?

What sort of information do the journalists want to know?

Which questions will they need to ask to find this out?

The journalists know that they have to interest the people who read their publications.

What sort of details would women's magazine readers be interested in? What about readers of current affairs journals? Sunday newspaper readers might like to know other details.

The different reporters will take turns to ask questions of the sailor.

THE SEA

THINGS TO MAKE AND DO

Make maps which show —
- A pirate's treasure island
- The school
- One section of the playground
- Your route from home to school

Let others use your maps to try to find their way around.

Make up some suitable names for pirates and pirate ships.

Play some sea games, e.g. 'The Sea and her Children', 'Shipwreck'.

Turn the room into a cave, an underwater scene, a ship.

Have a day when everybody comes dressed as a pirate.

Use seafaring terms for times in the normal school day, e.g.

playtime — eight bells
lunch time — mess time
home time — anchors away

Sing some sea shanties. What was the original purpose of these?

Find and read some stories and poems about famous ships and sailors. Read these to other people.

Say this quickly three times — 'She sells sea shells by the seashore'.

Invent exciting stories and poems about the sea.

Paint a sea scene on a window, or on a strong clear plastic sheet and tape it to the window. Write a sea poem on it.

Make fishing nets with paper and hang them up around the room. Fold the paper as if you are making a fan. Cut this way along the edges —

Be careful not to cut right through the paper. Open it out carefully and gently pull sideways. The nets could be decorated with cut-out paper fish.

Activities with water
Discover things that float and sink.
Make boats and hold boat races. How will you get your boat to move?
Try different ways to make waves and water currents.
Make an island in the water. Does this affect the waves and currents?
Use ice-blocks to make icebergs. What happens to the ice-block when you put it in the water?

Activities with sand
Build different sorts of sand castles.

Make a sand dune. Blow hard on it. What happens to the sand?

Take plaster casts of footprints, handprints, bike tyre tracks. Try and match them with the originals.

Dribble dry sand through your fingers. See how big a pile you can make.

Make some fish mobiles and hang them up.

Go to the beach

Be a beachcomber and collect anything of interest.

Can you identify all your objects? Can these be sorted or classified in some way?

Find the high water mark. How can you tell where it is?

Try and make the sea come up to the beach.

Count the waves. Is it true that every seventh is the biggest?

Make different sorts of tracks in the sand.

Make the biggest sand castle in the world.

Dig some holes and try to connect them with tunnels.

Write your name in the sand as large as you can or as small as you can.

Collect sea shells. What do you hear when you put a large shell against your ear?

Find out about

How sailors navigate across the sea.

How to use a compass.

What astronomy is.

The stars in the southern hemisphere.

What makes the sea salty.

What life was like in the convict transport ships.

READERS

Young Australia Language Development Scheme Nelson	**Stepping Stones** Books 4, 36
Methuen Caption Books Methuen	Orange 2 books
P.M. Story Readers Kea Press	Book 12c
Macdonald Starters Macdonald	4 books
Macdonald First Library Macdonald	6 books
The Signal Books Methuen	3 books
Australian People Longmans, Green & Co.	Books 1, 5, 20
P.M. Country Readers Kea Press	SP 11
P.M. Advanced Readers Kea Press	DE2, DE7, DE8
Cheshire Cat Cheshire	2 books
Lively Readers Nelson	2 books

THE SEA

Ladybird Wills & Hepworth	Series 536, 14, 21, 601	**Young Puffins** Penguin	19 books
Open Gate Oliver & Boyd	3 books	**Deep Sea Adventure** Wagner	8 books
Famous Ships Oliver & Boyd	4 books	**In History Series** Sims	4 books
Dolphin University of London Press	9 books	**Star Book** Hamish Hamilton	2 books
Topic Books Ginn	2 books	**Sea Hawk** Arnold	10 books
Griffin Arnold	20 books	**Starting Science** Chambers	3 books
Dragon Arnold	20 books	**Blackwell's Learning Library** Blackwell	7 books
True Adventure Blackie	9 books	**Let's Read And Find Out** Adam & Black	3 books
Trend Cheshire	4 books	**I Can Read Books** World's Work	9 books
Wide Range Series Oliver & Boyd	Green Book 1, 2, 3 Blue Book 1, 2, 3, 4, 5 Interest Book 1, 2, 3, 4 New Interest 1, 2, 4	**Bowmar Series** Bowmar	3 books
Scholastic Core Ashtons	26 books	**Discovery Project Kit — The Sea** Macmillan	13 books

MACHINES

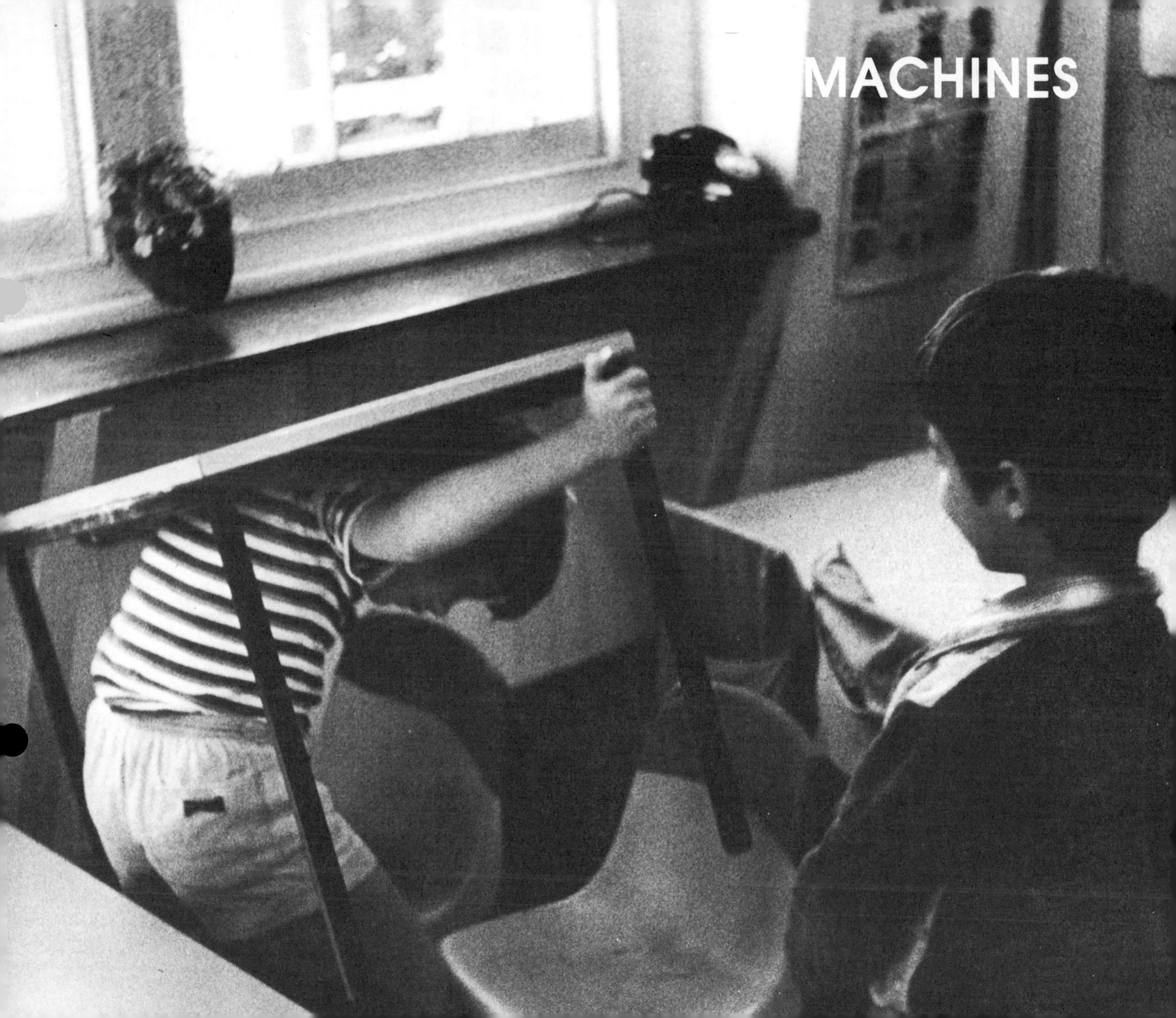

MACHINES

LISTENING ACTIVITIES

1 Children relax on the floor and close eyes.
Listen to the sounds that you can hear outside the room.
Pick a sound that you think is made by a machine. It might be a car, truck, train, earth-moving equipment or a drill.
Now quietly tell the person near you what you heard.

2 Close your eyes and listen to the sound of traffic. Pick one sound. What is it?
You are **in** this machine. Where are you going? Who is with you?
Tell someone near you what you are thinking.

3 Groups of four or five
The groups explore to find things in the room that could make machine-like sounds if rattled, scraped or bumped together.
These sorts of sounds might be heard in a factory. After each group has discovered and practised their combination of sounds, they take turns to make them for the other groups.
The others might like to suggest what type of factory the sound might come from.
Each group sound could be recorded on tape. This tape could then be used as a basis for rhythmic movement, e.g. a 'Machine Dance'.

Hint: If the group is a fair distance from the microphone, the individual sounds in the group blend together more and tend to become more machine-like.

4 An obstacle course is set up, using chairs, tables, desks, cartons, etc. These obstacles are the machines in a factory. All the children should agree on what type of factory it is.
Children then find a partner, and decide A and B.
A is the foreman of the factory. B is a blind visitor, and must close his eyes or be blindfolded.
A has to guide B through the factory, and make sure that B doesn't bump into or touch any of the dangerous machinery. A is allowed to direct B only by talking to him.

LOOKING ACTIVITIES

5 Mirror activity
Children find a partner and decide A and B.
A and B stand face to face about 1 metre apart.
The top half of A's body is a machine, and he starts it moving.
B is a mirror reflection of A, and he tries to do the same movements at the same time.

6 Variations of the mirror activity
With partners: B is a shadow of A. The shadow may fall beside, behind or on the floor in front of A.
In threes: A leads, and B and C are shadows.
In groups: There are six to eight children in a circle. The leader initiates the movement, and the others try to synchronise. No one in the group is allowed to turn his head to watch the leader. It should be possible to follow his movements by watching the person opposite.
(In all the above activities, the leader initiates the sound to go with the movements. The partner or group mirror both movement and sound.)

7 Children find partner and choose A and B.
A performs some movements that are used when operating or working with a machine, e.g. pulling a lever, twisting a wheel, pressing a button.
B watches, then copies A's movements.
A could make the appropriate sounds to go with the movement, which B would also copy.

8 A and B are waterside workers unloading a ship.
A is in the cabin of a crane which is high above the deck. B is in the hold of the ship.

What cargo is the ship carrying? How is this cargo packed — in boxes, bales, etc?
A and B are so far apart that they cannot hear each other, so have to communicate through signals.
When A has lowered the hook of the crane, B fastens the ropes around the cargo, checks that it is secure and signals A to haul it up.
What controls does A have to operate the crane?

MACHINES

TOUCHING ACTIVITIES

9 You are typing a letter to a friend. You are an expert typist, so you use all your fingers. How do you get the spaces between the words? What do you do if you make a mistake? When you have finished, find a friend and read your letter to him.

10 Your job in the factory is to keep two smooth surfaces well greased so that they slide together easily.
You have a large tin of special industrial grease, which isn't dirty, but is sloppy and squelchy and mucky to handle. You need a lot of grease at one time so you have to put it on in handfuls.
How does it feel?
Does it smell of anything?

11 Children find a partner, and decide A and B.
A has special power in his hands. He can cut through almost anything by merely sliding his hands across the surface.
B is a block of steel.
A is going to shape B into a life size human looking robot, by tracing around B's shape with his special hands.
How will A use his special power to make the features on B's face?

12 **'Toffee Machine'** Ten to twelve players. Circle formation with one person in the centre.
The person in the middle is the 'toffee' and closes his eyes. The 'toffee' bubbles around and tries to touch people in the circle. If touched, that person is turned into 'toffee', and must go into the centre

and close his eyes. Then both lots of 'toffee' try to tag other people. All the 'toffee' must stay stuck together in some way.
The game continues until all the players have been touched and turned into 'toffee'.

TASTING AND SMELLING ACTIVITIES

13 You are packing chocolates by hand in a chocolate factory. It is a very hot day, and the chocolates are soft.

Chocolate keeps sticking to your fingers but you don't mind at all!

How does the melted chocolate taste? Are you packing light or dark chocolate? Do they taste different?

14 With a partner

You are both official food-tasters in a canned fruit factory. Your job is to sample some of the tins of fruit to check that it is ripe and sweet enough.

What is the fruit? How does it taste?

Is there enough syrup with it?

What do you do after you have tasted it?

Do you have to make an official report?

15 With a partner

A is the owner of a small perfume factory. B is a buyer who is choosing perfumes for his business.

A shows B the perfumes, and B smells many different ones before he decides to buy.

What sort of perfume is B wanting?

Perhaps A has recently developed a new perfume that he is very proud of, and shows this to B.

16 Groups of four or five

Many different smells come from factories. In your group, try to work out the sorts of smells that would come from these factories. You might decide if they are pleasant or unpleasant smells, and if they remind you of anything.

- An incense factory.
- A tripe factory.
- A sugar cane processing factory.
- A leather treatment factory.
- A soup factory.

Where might these factories be found? What would the residents of the area think of the smells?

You might be able to think of some more factories, and the smells that would come from them.

MACHINES

EXPLORING MOVEMENT AND SOUND
(INDIVIDUAL ACTIVITIES)

17 All sit on the floor in a large circle. The teacher claps a short, simple rhythmic pattern, repeating it several times without stopping. The children join in when they know the pattern, until all clapping is synchronised.

This pattern is then transferred to other body parts, e.g. tapping on knees, head, shoulders, stamping feet in time, thumping on the floor etc.

Individual children could give other patterns, which would be treated in the same way.

18 Developing from the previous activity, the children could find words to fit the rhythm. Any suggestions would be tried out by clapping and chanting. The children to decide which one is most effective.

This may develop to a stage where everyone is stamping, clapping and chanting as they move around.

19 The teacher or child starts a rhythmic beat going on a tambourine, drum, or by clapping.

The children move in time to the rhythm, but use only their hands and arms. After a while, the leader nominates other parts of the body to move in time to the rhythm, e.g. hips, heads, feet, shoulders, knees, tongues.

Each of these might be treated separately, or combined with each other.

20 You are an operator of a hand forklift machine, unloading pallets from a truck. There are controls that make the forklift go forwards and backwards, and up and down.

Carefully manipulate the arms of the forklift into the pallets.

Take care as you lift the heavy load. Is it balanced? Move it off the truck and wheel it to where you are making your stack. Make sure you place it down gently.

How do you release the arms?

Now go back for another load.

21 You are driving a manually operated car.

Take care that you have a smooth start. Move through the gears as you pick up speed. Is the car running smoothly?

Traffic is heavy, so you have to keep alert. A slow truck is ahead. What do you do?

Don't forget to put on your indicator and check your rear vision mirror before you pull out.

22 You are driving a car when you notice smoke coming from under the bonnet! What will you do?

Perhaps you should stop.

When you lift the bonnet, you have a careful look at the engine. Can you see what the trouble is? Will you be able to fix it yourself or will you have to telephone for help?

23 You are a mechanic servicing a car.

Do you use a hydraulic hoist?

What do you do under the car?

Now you might check under the bonnet.

The car needs oil, and water in the radiator and battery. What about the tyres?

24 You are driving to a party in your best gear when you have a blowout.

What happens to the steering? You bring the car under control — you're a very skilful driver — and pull to the side of the road. Which tyre has blown?

Well, if you are to get to that party you'll have to change the tyre. Have you got a spare wheel and jack?

When you have changed the tyre, your hands are filthy. What can you do to clean up?

25 You are putting a machine together from all sorts of junk piled up around you. It may be any size, tiny, huge or medium.

Do you know what the machine is or are you just going to start and see what it becomes as you go along?

You have to fix the different parts together in many ways.

When you have finished, see if your machine works. Find a friend to show, and explain how it works.

Does your machine do anything in particular? What sound does it make as it works?

26 Radar game
Using just their voices and mouths, the children experiment to find repetitive machine-like sounds, e.g. bleeps, whistles, clicks, pops.

Each person selects one of their sounds, and repeats just that one.

All of these sounds come from a huge, moving machine, which is formed by the children kneeling on the floor, closing their eyes, and making their sound as they move around.

The aim of the game is that the children will move and make sound with their eyes closed, but not bump into each other. They will therefore be using all the sounds as 'radar'.

27 'Chocolate factory'
Good game for outside or in hall. You need a number of blocks or bean bags. Mark four areas on the ground. Divide the children into four equal groups. Each group stands around a marked out area. (factory). Bean bags represent the chocolates in the factories.

This game is activity oriented. The children take as many chocolates as they can — one at a time — from other factories, and put them into their own factory.

A signal from you on the tambourine will start and end the game.

28 You are riding your trail bike on your uncle's farm, helping him round up his sheep.

The paddock is bumpy, with rocks and dead trees scattered about. Some of the sheep keep breaking away in the wrong direction, and you have to herd them off.

Try and keep the flock together and moving.

MACHINES

29 You are a motor bike rider competing in a hill climb. Your bike is well tuned up, but while you are waiting your turn you might make some final adjustments to the engine.
Now you've had the signal to start. It's a very steep hill, and parts of the track are deep in mud.
Off you go! Good luck!

EXPLORING MOVEMENT AND SOUND
(PARTNER ACTIVITIES)

30 A works out a sequence of three movements with sounds to go with them, e.g.
a sideways bend — 'eeek'
a leap — 'zoooom'
a crouch — 'rrrrr'
A then teaches his sequence to B and both do it together, repeating it without stopping until the movements are rhythmic and synchronised.
The partners might be a machine, or part of one. If so, what is the job that the machine does?

31 A and B are steel robots unloading a truck stacked with boxes.
A lifts a box off the truck and passes it to B. B carries it, stacks it with the other boxes, and returns to get another one.
Are the boxes heavy?
How do the robots move?
Do they make a noise?

32 A is the operator of a scrap metal crushing machine. He has a remote control box with different levers and buttons which operate the machine.
B is the object being crushed. He might be an old car body, a refrigerator, an old stove.
A operates the machine which picks up B, moves him to the crushing site, and squashes him flat!
How does the machine sound as it works?
Is there any sound as the scrap metal is being crushed?

33 Magnets
A is a magnet and B is a metal toy, robot, car,

piece of machinery, perhaps with wheels on it.
As the magnet works, all or part of the metal object responds to the pull. The magnet could pull from different directions, e.g. behind, in front, from the side.

34 The pilot and passenger of a light plane are on a journey, when the engine starts to splutter and falter. They are forced to make an emergency landing, which is very bumpy and scary.
Where have they landed? Are they in mountains, desert, the bush or near the sea?
After inspecting the engine, they find that the trouble is serious. What can they do to fix it?
Perhaps they could adapt another part of the plane to repair the damaged part?
How do they feel about their situation?

35 Two bulldozer drivers have the job of clearing a paddock of trees. A length of strong chain is fastened between the bulldozers.
As they move, the chain drags along the ground between them, uprooting trees and bushes. It is very noisy and bumpy work.
The drivers will have to keep their bulldozers parallel in order to work efficiently. Be careful that the chain doesn't get pulled too tight.
What do the drivers do when the chain has collected a big pile of trees?

36 Two forestry workers are using a crosscut saw to cut down a huge tree. They will have to work rhythmically.

How can they help each other to keep in rhythm?
What sound does the saw make as it cuts the wood?
It is hard and tiring work, and sometimes they have to stop for a rest.
What do they do when the tree is almost cut through and about to fall?
What sound does the tree make as it crashes to the ground?

MACHINES

EXPLORING MOVEMENT AND SOUND
(GROUP ACTIVITIES)

37 Groups of four or five

This is a development from partner activity 30.
Each group combines to make one machine. It could be a real machine of practical use, a fantasy machine, or one that just moves!
The children will use their bodies, and make sounds appropriate to their movement.

38 Groups of four

Three people are the machine, one person is the operator.
The three develop the machine and it starts to work. Does it make a noise?
As the machine works, the operator supervises.
Something goes wrong, and the machine slows down and finally stops. The operator fixes the trouble and starts the machine again.
Everything runs smoothly for a while, but oh dear, the machine goes wrong again and begins to speed up. It gets faster and faster! The operator tries to fix it, but to no avail. LOOK OUT!

39 Groups of six to eight

Some members in the group are a machine that manufactures a certain product. The group will need to decide what the product is.
The remaining members of the group are the actual product being manufactured.
They will be fed in one end, processed through the machine, and emerge completed.

40 Groups of ten to twelve in a circle

All are operators around a huge circular machine.

Each operator is responsible for that part of the machine in front of him. He oils it, polishes it, checks the gauges and continually services the machine as it works. Each operator makes the sound of his part of the machine.

41 Groups of five or six

Each group are workers on the assembly line of a factory.
What is the product on the assembly line?
What is the task of each worker? Are all tasks different?
These are repetitive tasks, so the movements are repetitive and rhythmic.

42 Groups of five or six

The groups work together to make different kinds of machines, e.g.
- a machine that can fly
- a machine that goes underwater
- a machine that runs on rails
- a machine that measures time
- a machine that moves heavy loads
Sound effects would add interest.

TALKING ACTIVITIES
(PARTNERS)

43 A is a very sophisticated robot that has been specially programmed to respond to spoken commands.
B is its owner.
The owner gives the robot directions which it carries out.

44 A is a motorist who has gone through a red light.
B is a policeman who pulls A up.
Can A give any reason for his action?
Depending on the reason, what does B do? Does he give A a warning, a ticket, or a police escort?

45 A is a door-to-door salesman in sewing machines.
B is the house owner who is not very interested in buying a new machine.
A is keen to make a sale, so he keeps pointing out different features of this new model.
What objections or arguments does B raise for not wanting to buy?
How does A answer these objections?
How do they work it out?

46 A is the foreman of a factory machine-shop.
B is a new employee on his first day on the job. He will have the responsibility for operating a machine.
A explains to B how this machine works, what it makes, and how to operate it.
Does B understand immediately, or does he need to ask questions?
Are there any safety regulations which A should talk about before B starts work?

47 A is a steam train enthusiast who believes that this is the only way to travel.
B prefers electric trains.
What points does each one make to try and convince the other?
B might argue for speed, cleanliness and convenience.
A would have answers for that, and good reasons why steam trains are better.
Can they reach agreement?

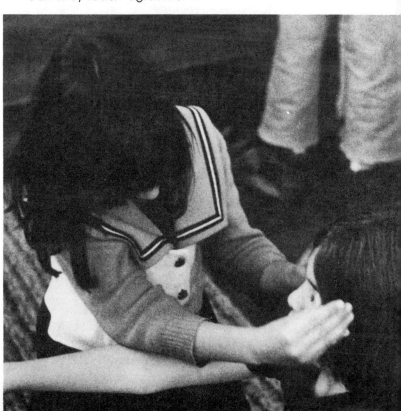

MACHINES

48 A thinks of a real machine, e.g. one used in a house, a factory, or for transport, and describes it to B **without naming it.**

A can tell B what it looks like, how it works, and even what it is used for, but never actually says its name.

B can ask questions, and tries to work out what the machine is.

49 You and your friend are at home alone and decide to surprise Mum by doing the washing. You are not too sure about how the washing machine operates, but you think you'll be able to work it out.

Some clothes are very soiled. What do you do about these?

Everything is going well, until you come to the spin-dry cycle. Then something goes wrong.

What happens? What do you do?

Can you fix everything up before Mum gets home?

50 Two friends on holiday are exploring an abandoned rocket launching site in the desert. They discover a strange looking object which is really huge, and appears to be some sort of machinery.

Together they talk about how it looks, and try to work out what it might have been used for.

Perhaps they can get it working. If so, what does it do, and what happens?

TALKING ACTIVITIES
(GROUPS)

51 Groups of four to six

One robot, its inventor, and several business people.

The inventor explains how his robot works and what it can do. He demonstrates with the robot just how clever it is.

The business people ask questions of the inventor, and ask to see the robot doing different tasks.

52 Groups of four to six

Talk about the number of machines that are in your houses. What are they?

Do you all have the same ones, or do some group members have different machines?

The group might like to draw them, or make a list or a graph.

53 Groups of five or six

Can you think of any jobs that were originally done by hand, but are now done by machines?

Here are some ideas —

Handwriting — typewriter

Hand lettering — printing press

Ploughing by hand — tractor

Think up some more.

What are the advantages of machines doing these sorts of jobs? Can your group think of any disadvantages?

Words like 'automation' and 'redundancy' are often used in relation to machines. Do you know what these words mean? How could you find out? Can you find out any other words of this type that relate to machines?

54 Groups of five or six

The group works together to design a strange machine which does a particular task.

It could be a funny machine, e.g. one that ties hair ribbons or one that smacks naughty children. It might be a machine that does your homework, washes the car, or weeds the garden.

The group could sketch and label their machine.

55 Groups of four to six

The teacher has prepared a number of cards with the names of three machines written on each one, e.g.

tractor	train	dishwasher
sewing machine	clothes dryer	pump
lathe	record player	aeroplane

These cards are placed face down in an accessible spot for all the groups.

One person from each group collects a card, returns to his group, and describes from the card each machine in turn, e.g. its size, appearance, how it works, but does not actually **name** the machine. The group is allowed to question the person with the card, and each member tries to work out the actual name of the machine on the card.

When the group has worked through all the machines on the card, it is returned to the pile, and another group member picks a new one.

Hint: It is a good idea to have twice the number of cards as there are groups, i.e. six groups =

twelve cards, because some groups will work out the machines very quickly.

Variation: The person with the card reads the name of the machine to the group. Each group member in turn describes some aspect of that machine, e.g.

Group leader — (reads) 'Train.'
1st member — 'It carries passengers.'
2nd member — 'It runs on rails.'
3rd member — 'It is very noisy.'
4th member — 'It can be powered by steam.'

MACHINES

THINGS TO MAKE AND DO

Collect pictures of machines. Photograph some in the neighbourhood, or collect them from newspapers or magazines.

Make a 'Mad Machine' book with drawings and explanations of how they work. Put them together to make a class book.

Use blocks, meccano, scrap materials to make real or fantasy three-dimensional machines.

Build a huge machine in one corner of the room. Nice or nasty things might happen when the machine works.

Find and read stories and poems about men and machines.

Make lists of machine words. Write these on cardboard cut out in machine shapes.

Make mobiles of machines, and hang them up around the room. Write the machine words on them.

Turn the room into a machine workshop. Make labels for the different activity areas.
Science table becomes   EXPERIMENTAL SECTION

Art area becomes   DESIGN SECTION

Maths area becomes   COMPUTER SECTION

Library becomes   RESEARCH SECTION

Experiment with printing techniques.

Discover and make lists and/or drawings of machines used in the home, in the school.

Select a well known machine, such as a car, and work on improving different features of it, e.g.
safety features
size and seating capacity
lighting system

Compare old and modern machines. What improvements have been made to old ideas? For example, in food storage; Coolgardie safe — icechest — refrigerator — freezer.

Find out about old machines that don't exist any more. Why don't they?

Try to find out about relatively new machine inventions that have occurred only because of modern living requirements, e.g. in the building industry.

Try and find out about any inventions that were designed by Australians and are now world famous, e.g. Shepherd castors.

Find out about
Solar energy machines
How cranes work
What a 'cherry picker' crane is
The factories in your neighbourhood
How a car engine works
How television works

READERS

Young Australia Language Development Scheme
Nelson — Stepping Stones Books 22, 25

Read To Yourself
Ginn — Book 3

Bobby Books
Reed — Book 6

P.M. Story Readers
Kea Press — Book 6a

In History Series
Sims — 4 books

Star Book
Hamish Hamilton — 3 books

Starting Science
Chambers — 2 books

Blackwell's Learning Library
Blackwell — 5 books

Machines At Work
Ginn — 6 books

Let's Read And Find Out
Adam & Black — 2 books

Open Gate
Oliver & Boyd — 2 books

Wide Range Series
Oliver & Boyd — Green Book 1, 2, 3, 5
Blue Book 2, 3, 4, 5, 6
Interest Book 1, 2, 3, 4
New Interest 1, 2, 3, 4

Dolphin
University of London Press — 5 books

Dolphin Science
University of London Press — 4 books

Reason Why
Dobson — 8 books

What Happens When
Oliver & Boyd — 4 books

Scholastic Core Libraries
Ashtons — 7 books

Young Puffins
Penguin — 5 books

Ladybird
Wills & Hepworth — Series 601, 606E, 654, 708

Macdonald First Library
Macdonald — 11 books

MACHINES

The Changing Scene Burke	3 books
Action Books Brockhampton	2 books
We Read About Heinemann	6 books
Junior True Books Muller	6 books
Topic Books Ginn	2 books
Penguin Primary Project Penguin	2 books
True Adventure Blackie	2 books
What Happens Hart — Davis	6 books
Signpost Library Oliver & Boyd	4 books
Lively Readers Nelson	2 books
Scott Foresman Systems	Levels 7, 9, 11

CIRCUS AND ZOO

CIRCUS AND ZOO

LISTENING ACTIVITIES

1 Relax on the floor and close your eyes.
I'm going to stand still, and rattle the tambourine.
Keep your eyes shut, and point to the sound.
Open your eyes. Are you right?
Close your eyes again. This time, I'm going to creep to another part of the room to make the sound. When you hear the sound, point to it.
(Teacher moves quietly to another spot in the room and makes the sound.)
Open your eyes. Are you right?
Close eyes again. You are all very clever mind readers who work in a circus. This time I'm going to move around so quietly that you will hardly hear me. Try and read my mind to work out where I'm going. Keep pointing to me as I move.
(Children do this. Finally teacher stands still and rattles the tambourine.)
Open your eyes. Were you right? How did you know where to point?

2 Animal Noises
What sort of sounds would be made by —
- a monkey which has hurt its paw?
- a hungry bear?
- a snake which is looking for another snake?
- a dog which is tied up, and has just seen a rat?
- an elephant which is trying to drag a caravan through thick mud?
- a pig with the 'flu?
- a dingo howling at the moon?

3 The teacher has a record or tape of a brass band playing marching music.

Children close their eyes and listen while the music is played. (About 20 seconds of music is ample.)
Where might this sort of music be heard? (Give the children time to talk about this.)
This time, the music is heard at a circus. Close your eyes, and work out what is happening. (Play the same piece of music again.)
The children could discuss in a group, or tell a partner what was happening in their circus.

4 Use percussion and tuned instruments such as xylophone, glockenspiel, chime bars. Children work in groups with the instruments to make either sounds or tunes to represent different animals, e.g. drum roll — lion; triangles — monkeys.
When they have worked out some sounds, or in five minutes (it will be noisy, but be patient!), all noise stops.
The teacher then makes up a simple story which involves all the instruments in turn. A simple start would be a waking-up-in-the-morning type story for a zoo, or a performance story for a circus.

Example: Circus story
Teacher: 'The monkeys were on first. They came into the ring, rolling and tumbling, and started their funny act.'
Children: Monkey noises on percussion.
Teacher: 'Then the monkeys waved as they left.'
Children: Stop monkey noises.
Teacher: 'Then came the lions!'
Children: Lion noises on percussion.
The children who weren't involved with percussion

at that moment, could close their eyes and 'see' what was happening in the act. They could then talk about this with others before the next act started.

LOOKING ACTIVITIES

5 Circus costumes are always very colourful.
Can you think of any reasons why this is so?
Look around the room to see if there are any colours that might be suitable for circus costumes. You could talk about these with a friend, and tell what colours you like, and which circus performer might wear them.

6 Can you see anything in the room that is the same shape as the circus ring? What have you seen?
Make this shape with your hands.
Can you make a circus tent with your fingers?
Make your hands move like an acrobat, twisting and tumbling.
Now you have the hands of a juggler.
What are you juggling? Is it big or small, heavy or light? Perhaps it is very smooth like a ball, or very dangerous like sharp knives?
Watch what you are doing. You don't want to have an accident!

7 With a partner
A is a make-up expert at the circus. He is creating a new face for a clown. He tries out many expressions in the mirror before deciding on one.
B is the reflection of A, and so mirrors all of A's expressions.
When A has found an expression he likes, he starts to apply his make up.
B continues to mirror A's actions.

8 With a partner
Look at your own hands. Animals have paws

35

CIRCUS AND ZOO

instead of hands. Show your partner your hands, and explain in what ways they are different from paws.

Where does the fur grow on a paw?

Are the nails the same shape as on your hands?

What does the underside of an animal's paw look like?

Are there any animals whose paws look like human hands?

9 People can tell how old a horse is by looking at its teeth.

What does this tell them?

What are they looking for? Have a look at your partner's teeth. How many teeth has he got?

Are there any gaps where teeth are missing?

Could this help you decide how old your partner is?

Does your partner have any fillings?

Do animals ever get toothache, and need to go to the dentist?

TOUCHING ACTIVITIES

10 With a partner

A has a collection of pieces of differently textured cloths.

B has eyes closed or is blindfolded.

A gives B a piece of material.

B feels it, then tells A what fabric it is (if he knows) or describes how it feels.

Then B suggests what circus costume could be made out of this material, e.g. chiffon could make a bareback rider's costume.

11 See if you can find something in the room that feels strong enough to form the centre pole of the big circus tent.

Can you test its strength in some way? Will it shift if you lean against it? Is it heavy enough to stand firmly? What happens if you pull at it?

Can you find something else that is stronger?

When you have decided on your centre pole, try and find a suitable fabric to make the tent walls. It should be fairly heavy, as it has to stay firm even in windy weather. Wander around and feel some different fabrics to see what is here.

What about fabrics in people's clothes?

What other things in the room remind you of a circus? How do they feel?

What could they be used for?

12 You are the owner and trainer of a world famous flea circus. The fleas can do all sorts of wonderful tricks, but they are so small!

The whole circus fits on to a space the size of a desk or table.

The fleas can't set up the circus, so you have to do it for them.

How do you arrange the circus site. Where does the tent go?

Do the fleas use any equipment such as trapezes, slack wires, catching nets?

These are really very tiny, so you have to be very careful.

When you have finished, show someone and explain why you have arranged it that way, and what tricks your fleas can do.

Is there an extra smart flea, which is the star of the show?

13 You work in the animal nursery at the zoo. Your job involves caring for the baby animals, making sure they are fed, and kept warm and happy.

You have been given a tiny, helpless little animal that needs a lot of cuddling.

It loves you, and likes to snuggle up to you while you stroke it.

What is it?

Is it furry, or fluffy, or prickly?

It is hungry, and keeps making little sounds.

What does it eat? How do you prepare its food?

TASTING AND SMELLING ACTIVITIES

14 There is a stall selling hot buttered popcorn just near the big top at the circus. The popcorn smells delicious, salty and buttery, and it is sold in big paper cups.

Do you have enough money?

When you try your popcorn, it is really hot, crunchy on the outside, and soft on the inside. It has just the right amount of salt and butter.

Mmmmm, doesn't it taste great?

15 **With a partner**

What sort of food can you buy at a circus or zoo?

How is it sold — in bags, cups, packets, on a stick?

A chooses one food to describe to B. He talks about its colour, taste, texture (crunchy, soft, smooth) smell, temperature (hot, cold, warm).

A tries to describe this food so vividly, that B's mouth waters just hearing about it.

16 You are a fire-eater at the circus. Part of your act is where you appear to breathe fire. To do this, you take a mouthful of highly inflammable liquid, slosh it around in your mouth, and spit it out. You then put a lighted match near your mouth, breathe out, and your breath catches fire. It is a most spectacular trick, but very dangerous and only for professionals.

Have you got your matches ready? Now take a mouthful of liquid. How does it taste?

Slosh it around in your mouth, and spit it out quickly. UGH!

Will your breath light?

How do you extinguish the flames?

CIRCUS AND ZOO

17 The baby zebra at the zoo has to have a certain formula in his bottle. Various things are to be added to his milk.
What are they?
Make sure you measure out just the right amounts.
How do you mix them together?
Does the bottle have to be warmed? How do you test if the milk is the right temperature?
How does the zebra's formula taste?

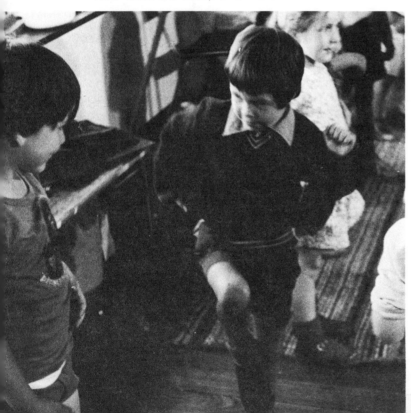

EXPLORING MOVEMENT AND SOUND
(INDIVIDUAL ACTIVITIES)

18 Curl up small on the floor.
You are the small grains of corn lying at the bottom of the popcorn machine. You lie there quietly, while the popcorn man turns on the heat.
The popcorn machine starts to heat up, and the corn sizzles in the butter.
What sound does it make?
(Start shaking the tambourine softly.)
It gets hotter, and the corn starts to swell.
(Louder sound with tambourine.)
Suddenly the corn pops.
(Big bang on tambourine.)
It explodes into big shapes.
What sound does the corn make as it pops?

19 You are a circus clown putting on your costume in preparation for the performance. Your costume is in a big box in front of you.
First you take out your big flat shoes. Put them on. They make you walk in a funny way.
Next you find your floppy pants. What colour are they? Put them on carefully over your shoes. They are really baggy and funny pants.
Now your clown's shirt. It has loose sleeves, and big buttons down the front. You have a ruffle in your box, that will fasten around your neck.
Do you have a hat? What does it look like? It might have pompoms, or feathers, or spangles.
How do you keep it on?
Now you are ready. Parade around in your costume, and show the others how fine you look.

(Beaut for littlies!)

20 You are a hungry giraffe at the zoo.
Feeding time is still hours away, but outside the high wall of your enclosure those tasty looking leaves might be within your reach.
They are very high, so you have to stretch your long neck.
No, that won't work. Try stretching your body as well — stretch your spine and your back.
You are still not tall enough, so stretch your legs too.
You are nearly there! Perhaps if you stretch your lips and your long tongue you'll reach those leaves.
Ahhh! You've got them.
Relax, and crunch them up. How do they taste?

21 You are washing an elephant.
How big is it?
What have you got to help you — bucket, soapy water, mop, ladder?
Where do you start?
Is the elephant naughty or cooperative? Does the elephant like being washed?
Don't forget its ears and feet. Give it a scrub.
How do you wash the soap off?

22 You are a clown with an open umbrella, a large balloon, and a very active pig on a string.
Try to keep the pig away from the balloon.
Can you manage all this?

23 You are the ringmaster announcing the next act in the circus. What is it?
How will you introduce it? You want to excite the audience about what is to come.
Can you use any really expressive words?
Remember the audience is spread out, so you will have to speak loudly and clearly.

24 You are cleaning out the bear pit at the zoo. It is a real mess, so you have to work hard with your broom.
What else do you use?
You might have to hose the floor, shovel up the manure, clean out the dirty hay. It's a pretty messy job, isn't it?
When everything is clean, and fresh hay is laid down, you have to let the bear back into its enclosure. This could be a bit tricky.
How do you manage?

25 You are a tightrope performer at a circus.
You start on the platform, then move out on to the wire. Be careful how you place your feet. The wire starts to sway.
Fight for your balance!
What happens?

26 You are a skilled bareback rider on your performing horse.
What costume are you wearing?
What do you put on your shoes so you won't slip while you are doing your act?
What breathtaking tricks can you do?

27 You are working with an elephant to put up the big top at the circus.

CIRCUS AND ZOO

Where is the best place for you to stand to direct it — in front of the elephant, next to its ear, behind it?

You must keep urging it along with your voice.

Do you use any special words which mean certain things to the elephant?

28 It has been a wet day at the zoo, and the leopard's coat is muddy and dirty.

How will he get it clean?

He uses his rough tongue to comb and groom his fur the same way as a cat does. He works slowly and carefully over the different parts of his body, licking and smoothing his thick fur into place.

What about the spaces between his claws?

How does the leopard wash his face and behind his ears?

29 Play the children some brass band marching music. Two minutes would be ample, just to highlight the type of music that brass bands play.

Then all have a discussion about the instruments used in a brass band, what they look like and how they are played. Photos or pictures showing different instruments would be useful.

We are all in a huge brass band. Decide which instrument you would like to play.

How do you hold it?

What sort of sound does it make?

When a band is on parade, how are the instruments arranged?

In what order do the musicians line up?

(You might need to help the children arrange themselves in formation. The order of instruments should be the children's decision, but all drummers, trumpeters, trombonists etc. would be clumped together.)

The music is played again, and all the children march around playing their instruments.

30 The circus Grand Parade is taking place.

All the animals are in the ring; horses, bears, dogs, lions, elephants, monkeys.

Which animal are you?

How do you move?

What sounds do you make as you parade around the ring?

(As a variation, try playing the brass band music while the Grand Parade is on.)

EXPLORING MOVEMENT AND SOUND
(PARTNER ACTIVITIES)

31 Two clowns are —
- Driving a car. Bits keep falling off. What do they do?
- Building a house. Is it timber or brick?
- Painting the house. What colour is the paint? Do they have a ladder?
- Cooking a meal. What are they cooking? Do they have any trouble?
- Sailing a boat. What sort of boat is it? Are the clowns good sailors?

32 Two circus maintenance men are driving in the tent pegs which keep the big top standing firmly. They are using sledge-hammers to force the big steel pegs into the hard ground.
You take turns to hit the top of the peg with your sledge-hammer. Try to get a rhythm going, as this will help your movement.
Do you make any sounds?
Time is short, so you have to speed up.
This is very hard work.
When you have finished, have a short rest before you move on to the next tent peg.

33 A is a very timid animal which has just joined the circus. Decide if you are a small or large animal.
B is the trainer.
How can the trainer get the animal's confidence and show that he can be trusted?
How does the animal react to the trainer?

34 A is a lion who has been returned to the jungle. He has spent many years in the zoo and so has forgotten how to hunt for his food.
B is a jungle lion who is teaching A the techniques of hunting in the wild.
What sort of things does A need to learn —
- Hiding in the long grass?
- Keeping very still and watching?
- Creeping silently up on the prey?
- Tearing meat off a carcass?
- Roaring to communicate with other lions?
Is A successful or does he have to practise a bit?
Can B give him any extra tips on how to behave?

35 A is the circus photographer who is taking some publicity photos for circus posters. His job is to get some interesting, eye-catching shots of the big star.
B is the star being photographed. Who is it? A trapeze artist, lion tamer, juggler, clown, magician, sword swallower, fire-eater?
B poses in different ways for A to photograph. Can A find some interesting angles? What about close-ups as well as long shots?

36 Two labourers are building a new zoo enclosure for the otters. They will have to work out what otters need in order to be comfortable, e.g.
- water to swim in
- rocks to climb and lie on
- a shelter to sleep in
- perhaps a fence is needed so that the otters won't get loose
What size are the otters? Will this affect the size of their enclosure?

CIRCUS AND ZOO

Can you include a few things for them to play on, so that they won't get bored? How about building a slide going down into the pool?

The labourers may need tools to build the enclosure, dig the pool and construct the sleeping shelter. There are some heavy rocks to lift. Can they help each other with these?

Otters like running water. What can the labourers do about this?

(GROUP ACTIVITIES)

37 Groups of six to eight

The lions in the zoo are feeling restless and uneasy. They can sense that something is wrong. They prowl up and down in their cage, glaring at each other, growling and snarling softly.

Then one lion bangs against the door of the cage, and it swings open. What does he do?

What do the other lions do?

What happens next?

38 Groups of four

Three performing dogs and one trainer.

The trainer is teaching the dogs a new trick. What is it? Is it a difficult trick or an easy one?

How does he reward the dogs when they do the trick successfully?

How do the dogs feel? Do they like the trainer? Do the dogs make any sounds?

How does the trainer talk to them?

Variations: Other animal training acts, e.g. horses, seals, monkeys, lions, tigers, bears.

39 Groups of six to eight

In the zoo kitchen it is the busiest time of the day, as the cooks prepare food for all the animals.

The lions and tigers need fresh meat which has to be cut and weighed, then put in big baskets.

Fruit and bread is for the monkeys.

What is suitable for the birds?

The giraffes, hippos and all the other animals have to have their food prepared as well.

Each cook takes responsibility for a certain type of food, and all work very hard.

40 Groups of five to six

A monkey family is in its enclosure at the zoo. There are some baby monkeys, their mothers, and a few big males.

Is there a boss?

Some monkeys might be playing, some eating and some grooming each other.

Then visitors arrive with peanuts to feed them.

How does each monkey act in order to be thrown a peanut?

How do they eat the peanuts?

41 Groups of twelve

Erecting the circus tent.

Nine children use their bodies to make the tent. They lie face down on the floor in a circle, with their heads to the centre, and hands joined.

Three children are the workers erecting the tent. They space out around the outside of the circle.

The workers haul on imaginary ropes, and the 'tent' rises slowly. The nine children keep their hands joined, and slowly come to a standing position with joined hands held high.

A large piece of fabric such as a double bed sheet or mattress ticking could be draped over the 'tent'. This could be placed when the 'tent' is in position, or before it starts to rise from the floor.

TALKING ACTIVITIES
(PARTNERS)

42 Some animals are found in zoos but not in circuses. Can you work out which animals they might be? Why aren't they in circuses?

Why do we have zoos anyway? Who decides which animals are kept in zoos?

43 What sort of acts would you like to see in a circus? You might like to invent some new ones that would be exciting, or use some that you already know.

If you are inventing a new act, try to work out what people or animals are involved, the details of what happens in the act, and find a title for it which could go on a written programme.

Perhaps you could draw up this programme, trying to plan plenty of variety for the audience.

44 A and B are the same kind of zoo animal — bears, buffalo, penguins, etc.

A has been at the zoo for many years. He knows the routine of life in his enclosure.

B is a new animal who has just been captured and placed in the same enclosure.

What can A tell B about life at the zoo? He might show B around their enclosure, tell him about feeding time, visitors, how the humans treat animals.

Is there anything that A should warn B about?

45 A is the manager of a local circus.

B is a performer who has developed an unusual and spectacular act which he thinks should be included in the show.

B explains his act to A, giving reasons why it should be included.

CIRCUS AND ZOO

A might ask questions about any extra equipment B will need; whether anyone else is involved in the act; how much performing time it will take etc.
How does B answer these questions?
Depending on the answers, what does the circus manager decide?

46 You both work as Education Officers in the zoo school. Your job is to talk about the animals to children who come on excursions to the zoo.
Today you have a group of six-year-olds, who want to see all the animals that are native to Australia. They can only stay one hour, so you have to plan a timetable for them which will enable them to see as much as possible in that hour.
Which native animals are kept in your zoo?
Little children like baby animals. Are there any baby possums, wombats or dingo pups?
Will the children be allowed to play with these?
What sort of things could you tell them about the animals? You might have to keep it simple, because the children are quite young, and won't understand anything too complicated. Make sure your timetable isn't too tiring for the children.

47 The Australian Government has decided to give two kangaroos to a zoo in San Francisco, America.
You are both in charge of transporting these animals. They are to be air-freighted from Melbourne to San Francisco, and the flight will take about twenty-two hours.
What will you have to plan for this job?

How will you get the kangaroos to the airport? Will they travel in some sort of box or crate? If so, how big should it be? What will it be made of? If not, how could the kangaroos be prevented from moving around on the plane? Do you think they should be drugged for the flight so that they will be quiet, or is this too cruel?
What about food and water for the trip? Can you work out any other things that should be considered?

TALKING ACTIVITIES
(GROUPS)

48 Groups of six

What are the differences between a circus and a zoo?

Three children work on the circus, and three children on the zoo.

Each group thinks up a characteristic of a circus or zoo, and tells it to the other group —

Group 1 'Circuses use trained animals.'

Group 2 Tries to get a contrasting point, e.g. 'Zoo animals are not trained.'

Group 1 'Circuses move around a lot.'

Group 2 'Zoos are always on the same site.'

This could be varied by having groups of seven — six talkers and one scribe, who would write down the differences mentioned by the groups. Later, each group list could be shared with others, to make a composite list of all points.

49 Groups of three

A is the compere of a national television show. A segment of the show concerning animals, is being taped in the T.V. studios.

B is a zoo attendant who has brought an animal into the studio to show and talk about it on T.V.

C is the animal. What is it? Is it small or large? How is the animal feeling? Is it relaxed, or nervous? The compere asks questions about the animal, which the zoo attendant tries to answer. He may use the animal to demonstrate different points. Does anything funny or exciting happen?

50 Groups of four to six

Oral story making, 'What would happen if . . .' starting points. These could be suggested by the teacher or children.

Some suggestions

What would happen if —

- The circus tent was blown down in the middle of a performance?
- The lions escaped from the zoo?
- All the circus animals refused to perform?
- The trapeze artist broke her leg?
- The flea circus met a dog?

These topics and others could be discussed with the whole class first, and then the children could divide into groups to work out their stories.

51 Groups of four or five

You are a group of circus people who have bought thirty seconds of time on commercial television. You are going to use this time to advertise the circus. Work out a really effective commercial.

Will it have singing in it? If you are going to use circus characters, will they be in costume? What about make-up? Remember it is for colour T.V.

What message can you get across in thirty seconds?

52 Groups of four

Design a poster to attract people to your circus. What information will it need to show? (Place, time, name of circus etc.)

A few meaningful eye-catching words could be effective. What about layout and design? Are colours important?

CIRCUS AND ZOO

53 Groups of five to six

Group discussion on taking risks.

Some general questions which would start the talking, would be —

- What makes circus acts thrilling? (People take risks and do things that untrained people cannot.)
- Do you know any other job, not involved with a circus, where people take risks of this type, e.g. stunt men, kite men, stunt flyers, motorbike riders? Are the risks, that those people take, greater or less than those taken by circus performers? In what ways?
- Why do you think people get involved with this sort of job? What is the attraction?

54 Groups of five

You are a group of architects working on a plan for a new zoo. The site has already been decided, but you have to work out the plans for the grounds.

Where will the different enclosures go?

Are there any animals which should be kept away from others?

How much space will each enclosure take up? Will large animals need more space than small ones?

What about trees, rocks and sleeping shelters for each enclosure?

Plan picnic and garden areas for visitors.

The group may wish to sketch out their plan. Later they could share their ideas with others.

55 Groups of six

Four members of a family are being interviewed by the local circus manager and his deputy, about joining the circus.

The family explains their act, and tries to persuade the other two that they would be an asset to the circus.

The manager and deputy ask questions, and should try to reach a decision about employing the family, in about five minutes.

Variation:

Same situation, but the circus family have something to hide, and try to keep it from the local owners. What is it? (They are wanted by the police; they have had a run of bad luck; they haven't really perfected their act, but pretend they have.) In the interview, do the circus owners get an inkling that something is wrong, or not?

HINT

When organising this, it would be more effective if the circus owners did not know that the family has something to hide. They could be sent off to frame their questions before the family are told that they have this secret. Later, children could discuss if the owners found out, and how effectively the family kept their secret.

THINGS TO MAKE AND DO

Have a pet show at school. Arrange for the pets to be delivered and picked up at appropriate times.

Weigh the pets, measure them and make graphs. Use a stopwatch and time how long they take to do things, e.g.

crawl across the room

drink milk or water

eat a leaf.

Make graphs and write about the pets' favourite food.

Use percussion to compose animal tunes.

Pretend to be an animal for the day.

Collect things that come from animals or feel like animals, e.g. fur, feathers, bone, teeth, velvet material, hessian material, fur fabric.

Make animal paper bag masks with a supermarket bag. Cut holes for eyes and decorate.

Paint, draw, make or model a weird and wonderful fantasy animal. Make it **large**.

Visit the zoo

Find out how the native Australian animals are housed.

Notice the different enclosures for the different animals. Why is this so?

What does the zoo do to make the animals feel at home?

Get a map of the zoo (or make one). Try and discover why the zoo is planned in this way.

Have an 'Animal of the Day'. During the day, find out as much as possible about it.

Make dioramas of an enclosure at the zoo.

Erect a tent in the school grounds.

Hold your own circus.

Paint clown faces on balloons.

Make up your own face like a clown.

Make an insect zoo.

Find out the correct biological names for different animals.

Go on a tiger hunt around the school grounds.

All combine to paint a class picture of a circus or zoo on a huge sheet of paper.

Visit a circus

Find out how many seats there are in the big top.

Collect some advertising posters.

Talk to some of the people who work at the circus.

Find out how many years the circus has used the same site.

Find out what circus people do in the winter.

CIRCUS AND ZOO

Find out about
How to keep a dog.
What an elephant eats in a day. Compare this to
what you eat in a day.
Who Grock was.
Camouflage.
The evolution of the modern horse.

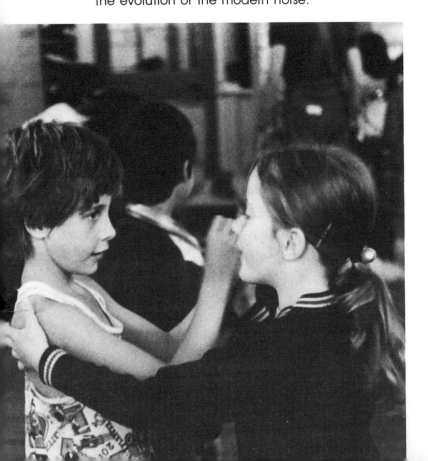

READERS

Young Australia Language Development Scheme Nelson	Readers No. 2, 4 Stepping Stones Books 6, 10, 15, 16, 35
Collins Mini Books Collins	Step 2 Book 1
Round and About Books Oliver & Boyd	3 books
Ready, Steady, Rhythm Readers Holmes	Book 3g
Reads Springboard Readers Reed	Book 8 Book 10
P.M. Story Readers Kea Press	Book 5d
Bruna Books Methuen	2 books
Flap Books Chatto & Windus	1 book
The Signal Books Methuen	3 books
Reading Systems Scott Foresman	Level 4H

WITCHES AND GHOSTS

LISTENING ACTIVITIES

1 Children relax on the floor and close their eyes. Listen to the sounds that you can hear inside the room. Pick a very soft sound and try listening only to that.

2 Keep breathing normally, and listen to the sound of your own breathing.
Now try to hear the sound of your heart. Can you feel your heart beat?
Show others what you do to feel your heart. How do their hearts feel?

3 Try and find some things in the room that make mysterious sounds. Perhaps they will be soft, scraping sounds, or creaking or rustling sounds. Show and tell someone what you found.

4 Children find a partner, and decide A and B.
A is the ghost. B is the person.
B closes his eyes.
A moves around using objects in the room to make sounds, e.g. crackling paper, tapping on window. B tries to work out what the 'ghost' is doing, and how he is making the sounds.

5 A is a mischievous ghost. B is a blind person and closes his eyes or is blindfolded.
A moves away from B, then starts to call his name.
B tries to reach and touch A, while A tries not to be touched. A may move, but must keep calling B.

Variation
A makes sounds instead of saying B's name.

6 A and B have been put under a spell by a witch. A can only speak in a whisper, and B cannot open his eyes.
A and B stand facing each other about one metre apart. A whispers instructions to B, e.g. 'scratch your nose, touch the floor'. B follows the instructions.
B moves around the room. A goes with him, trying to warn B about obstacles in his way.

LOOKING ACTIVITIES

7 One spooky thing about ghosts is that you can sometimes see through them.

Try and find some things in the room that you can see through. You might find something clear like a window, or cloudy, like curtains or sheer fabric. Can you find anything coloured that you can see through?

Try looking at people and objects through what you have found. Do they look different?

Talk to someone about what you are discovering.

8 Children find a partner and decide A and B. A is a witch. B is under the witch's spell. A does witch-like movements, and B copies.

9 Using a light source such as a candle, torch, lamp, projector or spotlight, the partners work together to cast shadows which remind them of witches or ghosts. They could use their whole bodies, or parts such as hands, heads.

After experimenting, some partners might like to make up a 'shadow story' using the shapes combined with spooky sounds. By trying this out, partners will discover which light source is most effective and why, and if there is a need to darken the area in which they are working.

10 Ghost Shapes

Partner game for outside on a sunny day.

A has a piece of chalk or a stick.

B makes his own shadow into a spooky shape.

A draws around the shape on the ground, then B moves away, and the outline is left.

A then tries to make his shadow fill the outline on the ground.

Partners could then wander around trying to make their shadows fit into shapes drawn by other partners.

11 Ghost Magic

Groups of eight to ten in a circle.

Several objects are placed in the centre of the circle, and the group examines them.

All close their eyes, and the teacher or group leader selects a 'ghost' by touching him.

Then the group, still with their eyes closed, count aloud and slowly up to ten.

The chosen ghost makes some objects 'disappear' by removing them, 'appear' by adding some, or rearranges those in the centre.

After counting, the group opens their eyes, re-examines the objects, and talks about the changes.

The group has three guesses to discover the 'ghost'. If correct, a new ghost is chosen. If incorrect, the same ghost has another turn.

TOUCHING ACTIVITIES

12 You are all under a witch's spell, and cannot open your eyes. Move around slowly. If you touch someone, try and discover who it is before you move on. Keep your eyes closed.

13 You gradually wake up in the middle of the night feeling really cold. You try to work out why. The window is closed, and you have three blankets on your bed, but you still feel cold. The air gets colder and colder.
Then slowly, a corner of your room fills with a glowing blue light.
(Begin to speak in a low, whispery voice.) It starts to take shape and spreads across the room towards you.
You are so scared that you shut your eyes tight and freeze where you are.
The thing oozes up on to your bed and touches your feet. How does it feel? Is it heavy or light; freezing cold or burning hot?
After a moment you feel it creep further . . . up your legs . . . then to your waist . . . your chest . . .
Then suddenly (loud bang on tambourine) . . .
What happened?
Tell someone near you about it.

TOUCHING ACTIVITIES
(PARTNER)

14 A's face has been changed by a witch, and everything is in the wrong place. Perhaps A's ears are on his chin, and his nose is in the middle of his forehead!
B puts A's face back the right way, making sure that everything is firmly stuck on.

15 A is a mischievous ghost.
B is a blind person, and so closes his eyes or is blindfolded.
A spins B around a few times, then B tries to go to the door. A tries to prevent B from getting there, but may not hold him. A is allowed to put things in B's way, and distract him by touching him lightly, making sounds, and talking to him.
When B gets to the door, the partners change roles.

16 A closes his eyes.
B finds something in the room that is soft to touch, e.g. a strand of knitting wool, the edge of a curtain, a jumper. B brushes this thing across A's face, and A tells him what witch-like or ghost-like thing it could be. For example, the strand of wool could feel like a spider's web in a witch's house.

17 Groups of three
A physically moulds B into the shape of a witch doing a certain task, e.g. riding a broomstick, casting a spell, dancing around the cauldron.
When A is finished, C observes B, then makes himself into the same shape.
A examines both, to check they are the same.

WITCHES AND GHOSTS

TASTING AND SMELLING ACTIVITIES

18 Find things in the room that have an unpleasant smell.
Are these smells strong or faint? Can you find some of each?
Do these smells remind you of anything?

19 As you are exploring in an old empty house, you open a cupboard and find a strangely shaped bottle of glowing liquid. You take the top off and smell the liquid, then dip your finger into it. You cautiously lick your finger.
As you taste the liquid . . .

20 You are exploring an old street in a strange city and feeling very hungry. You come to a shop that has food you have never seen before. How does it look and smell?
You want to know what the different foods are. What does the shopkeeper tell you? What do you decide to buy?
After you have chosen some food, the shopkeeper does not want money for it, but asks you for something else. What is it? Are you prepared to give it to him? What is he going to use it for?

21 With a partner
Make up a magic potion. What sort of things go in it? How long does it need to cook?
How does it taste and smell when it is cooked?

22 With a partner
You and your friend are trying a recipe that you found on a scrap of paper in your grandmother's recipe book. Some ingredients seem strange.

Can you find them all?
What do you think of them?
The mysterious recipe is finished and it looks a bit like stew. Your father is hungry, and wants his dinner quickly, so you decide to give him some of the stew. As he starts to eat . . .

EXPLORING MOVEMENT AND SOUND
(INDIVIDUAL ACTIVITIES)

23 You are a witch brewing up a magic potion in your cauldron. What goes in the potion?
How much of each ingredient do you use?
As you put each ingredient in, give it a stir with your large spoon.

24 You are a witch dancing around your cauldron.
Make up a magic spell to chant as you dance.

25 You are a witch on a journey at night.
How do you travel?
Where are you going?
Do you have anything with you?

26 You are a young ghost who is practising scaring people. You haven't done much of this before, so you need to try out many different movements and sounds to find the ones that are really scary.
When you have a good one, try it out on someone to see if it scares them.

27 In the haunted house the clock strikes midnight, and the ghosts wake up.
They begin to slowly come out of their hiding places, stretching and yawning, and start to drift and float around.
What do they do next?

28 You have received a pair of shoes in the mail without knowing who sent them.
You try them on and they fit perfectly.
But you soon find out that they are not ordinary shoes. They are magic!

What do they make your feet do?

29 You are the ugly, nasty, creepy-crawly things that a witch uses to make her magic potion. You roll and slither, tumble and creep towards the cauldron.
You crawl up the side, tumble in, and start to bubble and boil.

30 The teacher is the 'witch' who can change the children into anything she likes.
The children become that animal or thing, moving and making appropriate sounds until the 'witch' changes them to something else.
Suggested changes could be —
• animals (domestic and wild, small and large)
• birds and insects
• different people
• objects

31 The children move freely about the room. The teacher explains that when she makes a sound (bang on the tambourine) that they are in the 'witch's' power, and can move only in the ways the 'witch' commands. Some commands could be —
moving slowly
moving backwards
moving on one foot
moving close to the ground
moving in a circle
making a twisty path

Children could take turns at being the witch.

WITCHES AND GHOSTS

32 Witches' Cauldron

A chase and capture game for outside or in a hall.

Three witches are chosen, and their three cauldrons marked out by big chalk circles on the ground.

The rest of the class are creatures that the witches use as ingredients for the magic potions.

Each child decides what creature he will be, e.g. toad, frog, cat, bat, snake, lizard, and moves only as that creature moves.

The witches have to capture the creatures, take them to their cauldrons, and put them in.

When a witch touches a creature, it is under her spell and must do as she commands. Once a creature is in the cauldron, it cannot escape, but bubbles and boils, while making its creature-like sounds.

The game is finished when all the creatures are in the cauldron.

Variations

The witch can only move in a certain way, e.g. backwards, hobbling or limping, or in a crooked line.

The witch can only capture a creature if she touches a certain part of the body, e.g. back, shoulder, foot, hip.

EXPLORING MOVEMENT AND SOUND
(PARTNER ACTIVITIES)

33 Two young ghosts are playing in a deserted fun-park.

What is there to play on? (Get a few quick suggestions from the children, e.g. big dipper, ferris wheel, mad mouse, slide etc.)

Remember that the fun-park is closed, so if the ghosts want a ride on something like the big dipper, they might have to use some magic to make it work. How will they do this?

Do they ride on them the way that humans do, or do ghosts like to do things differently? Perhaps they enjoy creeping under things, climbing through them or jumping off them.

The ghosts are having great fun. What does a ghost laugh sound like?

34 The old witch is teaching the young one the movements and steps of a magic dance.

When the young witch has learned the dance, the old witch teaches her the magic words that go with the movements.

35 A is an old cat that has been with a witch for many years and is soon to retire.

B is the young cat who is going to take over.

The old cat shows the young one what a witch's cat should do, e.g. crouch and hiss, walk proudly, balance on the broomstick, creep quietly on roof-tops, communicate to the witch in cat language. The young cat copies the old one.

36 A is the witch who can change people into other things.

B is the person under the witch's spell.

The witch chants and dances her magic spell. She can use real words or made up ones. At the end of her chant she says what B is to become, e.g. cat, lion, frog, mouse, snake.

B turns into that creature, moving and making sound until the witch changes him into something else, or back to a person.

37 A is a very cheeky, naughty, little boy who has made his parents so angry, that they have locked him in his room.

B is the ghost that haunts that room.

The ghost tries to frighten the boy by making noises, floating about, and looking scary.

Is the boy scared? He is a very cheeky boy, so he might try to scare the ghost away.

What happens?

38 Two ghosts have frightened away a family of humans who were just about to have dinner. The food is on the table, and the ghosts are curious to try it.

What happens when they go to pick up something?

What can they do about this?

Can they help each other get something to eat?

WITCHES AND GHOSTS

EXPLORING MOVEMENT AND SOUND
(GROUP ACTIVITIES)

39 A group of ugly old witches are preparing to take part in a "beauty" competition to find the ugliest witch.

They will be judged on many different aspects; clothing, appearance, broomstick and wand, power and number of spells.

As they get ready, they practise their cackles and screeches, and quietly mutter their magic spells. They are jealous of each other, and each one wants to look better than all the rest.

40 Groups of eight to ten

You will need a length of fabric for each group. Half the group works together, using their bodies to make one abstract shape. Elbows and legs could give the shape different pointed parts. Arms and backs could make interesting curved parts.

When the shape is ready, the other half of the group drapes a large piece of fabric over the shape. Old sheets and curtains of different weights and textures would be suitable, or lengths of soft, fine material. (Look in the dress-up box.)

Now we have half the group making a covered shape that looks interesting, and might even look spooky!

What can happen now? The shape might change slowly to another one.

It might make different spooky sounds.

The group members outside the shape could pat or poke different parts, to see and hear what will happen.

What would it be like if the room was darkened, and torch light was played over the shape?

41 Change It

Groups of five or six in a circle.

The teacher gives each group an object which could be used for many different things.

Suggestions: stick, scarf, necklace, belt, ribbon, ruler, length of chain, embroidered tape, length of material.

One member starts by using the object as a prop for doing a certain task or movement. Sound must also accompany the action.

The rest of the group has to guess what that person is doing.

Examples:

Using ruler, make stirring motions, accompanied by 'mmm, yum, yum', and much smacking of lips. This might be mixing a cake.

Using scarf, make it into a sling and put arm in. 'Ooh, ouch, aah'. Arm could be broken.

Using chain, fix it to collar of imaginary dog. 'Here boy, heel', and whistling. Taking dog for a walk.

The group member who correctly guesses what is happening, has the next turn.

Hint: Limit the group size to a maximum of six, because it can get very boring waiting for a turn if the group is too large.

TALKING ACTIVITIES
(PARTNERS)

42 Have you ever been really scared by something? Take turns to tell your friend about it.

43 Two ghosts are talking about what they do to scare humans.
Do they have any favourite tricks that always scare people?
Does each one have different tricks?

44 This morning when you woke up, you both found you were invisible.
How did this happen?
Perhaps it was something you ate. Find out if you both had the same thing for dinner last night.
Perhaps it was something you both touched. Find out about that.
Did you both unknowingly chant a magic spell that made you invisible? If so, can you remember the words?
Sometimes if you say spells backwards they work backwards, and you might become visible again.
Does being invisible feel different?
Are there any good things about being invisible?
What are some bad things?
(This activity could be an effective lead in to some creative story-writing.)

45 A is a fortune teller.
B is having his fortune told.
A could use different methods of telling B's fortune
• reading the palm of B's hand
• reading the bumps on B's head
• reading the lines on B's face

46 A is under a witch's spell. He cannot speak English, or any other known language, but uses words that he makes up as he goes along.
A tries to explain to B in his made-up language, how the witch put him under this spell.

47 A is a fierce ghost who always scares adults.
B is the child who questions the ghost about why he likes to scare adults, and what it is like to be a ghost.

48 A is the Frog Prince who has been changed back to a human.
B is a member of his family.
B questions A about what it was like to be a frog.
Perhaps A will be able to tell B the best and worst things about being a frog.

49 Partners make up a witch's dictionary of magic words. These could be written down.

50 Make up some magic potion recipes. What ingredients might be in a recipe to —
• make people's eyes shiny?
• make a cat's fur fluffy?
• turn a person's skin blue?
• make an angry person happy?

51 Two ghost bosses are having a meeting to decide some 'Rules for Scaring' for the ghost community. Perhaps they make rules about the time, place, and way that humans should be scared. They may need to write down these rules.

TALKING ACTIVITIES
(GROUPS)

52 Groups of four

One witch and three people.

The witch can grant one wish.

The three people take turns to tell their wish to the witch, giving reasons why it should be granted.

The witch listens to all the wishes and reasons, and then decides which one she will grant.

The witch must also give reasons for her decision.

53 Groups of four, five or six

Astrology is the name of the science which uses star signs to predict the future. These star signs can be found in newspapers and magazines.

Work out the star signs for your group, by finding out everyone's birthday.

In your group, discuss whether or not this way of predicting the future is accurate. Try to give some reasons.

54 Groups of four, five or six

A group of good witches have the power to change things about our way of life, to make a better world. Work out some things that you would change.

Give reasons why the changes would be desirable.

What results would these changes have?

The group could write a list of their proposed changes.

55 Groups of four, five or six

Superstitions have been built up by people over hundreds of years.

Some things are believed to be lucky, and some unlucky.

In your group, talk about these superstitions, and try to work out —
- if they bring good luck or bad luck
- why people think this
- how these superstitions might have developed (the story behind them)

Examples

Having a horse shoe.

Walking under a ladder.

The number 13.

A four leaf clover.

Having a rabbit's foot.

Spilling salt.

Touching wood.

Putting shoes on a table.

Putting up an umbrella inside.

Seeing a white horse.

Touching a Chinaman.

Walking on the cracks in the footpath.

Find out good luck and bad luck beliefs which come from other countries.

Do you know any rhymes that are good luck chants?

WITCHES AND GHOSTS

THINGS TO MAKE AND DO

Make a huge witch's cauldron.

Look in a magazine to find star signs.

Turn the room into a witch's house, a haunted castle, a spooky cave.

Find some spooky stories and poems and read them to others.

Make up some spooky stories and poems of your own.

Make witches' broomsticks.

Make black cat mobiles. Cut out a cat's head from thin black cardboard. Cut a spiral from a square of black cardboard. This is the tail. Staple the tail to the bottom of the head. Thread some string through a hole between the cat's ears. Hang the cats up. They will turn slowly in the breeze.

Write a letter in invisible ink. If you don't know how to make it, try lemon juice.

Make a class book of spells.

Make lists of words to do with witches and ghosts. Write them on charts shaped like witches and ghosts, and hang them up.

Weave a huge spider web with black wool across one corner of the room. Decorate with spiders, bats and insects.

Make a witches' recipe book.

Practise some magic tricks. Try them on people.

Have a 'Spook Night'.

Try and find out if witches do exist.

Make some candles.

Make a life-size model of a witch, a wizard or a ghost.

Make witches' hats. Decorate with magic symbols.

Have a day when everyone dresses up as witches or ghosts.

Make some shadow puppets of witches.

Make magic pictures.
Fold a piece of paper in half.
Open it, and colour it heavily with lumber crayons on one side.

Close it again. Use a sharp pencil or biro to draw a picture on the front.

Open it again and see what has happened.

Work some magic with paint.
Start with only three primary colours — red, yellow and blue.
Mix them in different combinations, to make other colours.

See how the world changes when you look at it through coloured cellophane.

Make a sun dial.

Find out about
Tarot cards
Different ways of fortune telling
Fairies, gnomes and goblins
Faith healing
Invisible ink
Fairy rings
Hypnosis

WITCHES AND GHOSTS

READERS

Young Australia Language Development Scheme
Nelson — Readers 10, 16, 24

Ready, Steady, Rhythm Readers
Holmes — 1g, 2g

Bruna Books
Methuen — 4 books

Rigby's Reading Development Scheme
Rigby — 1 book

Breakthrough To Literacy
Longman — 2 books

Reading Systems
Scott Foresman — Level 3A, 3C, 3E, 3H, 4F, 5C

Wide Range Series
Oliver & Boyd — Green Book 1, 2, 3 / Blue Book 1, 2, 3, 4

Scholastic Core
Ashtons — 116 books

Young Puffins
Penguin — 97 books

Knight
Brockhampton — 10 books

Piccolo
Pan — 6 books

Armada
Collins — 4 books

Dolphin
University of London Press — 4 books

Trend
Cheshire — 1 book

FLIGHT

FLIGHT

LISTENING ACTIVITIES

1 Aeroplanes are made of metal. If you thumped an aeroplane, what sound would you hear?
Try to find some metal things in the room that make the same sort of sound when you thump them.

2 Balloons, kites and gliders need wind to help them fly. Using your mouths and voices, make the sound of a gentle breeze which is just enough to keep a balloon in the air.
Slowly the wind gets stronger. It is now blowing hard enough to toss kites around.
Soon the wind is strong enough to lift a glider into the sky.
Gradually the strong wind drops away, back to the gentle breeze. Then all is still.

3 As you are working in your garden, you hear the sound of an aeroplane flying overhead. Can you tell by the sound what sort of a plane it is?
You keep working, but then realise that you can hear the engine spluttering, stopping and starting, and a high pitched whine is getting louder. It sounds like the plane is in trouble! Tell someone near you about what is happening. How does it end?

4 With a partner
A is a model plane which can respond to spoken instructions.
B is the owner of the plane.
B gives instructions to A, e.g. 'dive, wings level, swoop, left turn, go straight'.
A obeys the instructions.

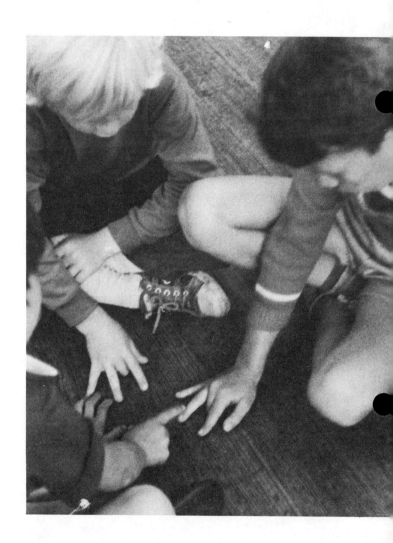

LOOKING ACTIVITIES

5 Look at the palm of your own hand.
Your palm is the ground seen from an aeroplane in flight. The lines on your hand might be rivers or roads. Where do they go? What else can you see?
Tell someone near you.

6 Look around the room at different colours.
Pick out some that you like, and tell someone near you about them.
You are an interior decorator who works for a big airline company. Your task is to decorate the inside of the new improved jet passenger plane.
Will you go for restful muted colours, or do you prefer something brighter?
Talk about your ideas with someone.

7 Feathers of birds are many different colours.
Look around the room, and see if you can find some colours that are also in birds' feathers. What birds are you thinking of?
Perhaps you might make up a bird which has gloriously coloured plumage. Talk to someone about it.

8 You are a signwriter painting the emblem of an international airline company on the tail of a plane.
What colours are you using in the design?
Trace the design before you start to paint.
Do you use fine brushes or thick ones? Take care that you keep inside the lines you have drawn.

9 Partners
A is directing a plane landing on an aircraft carrier. (Mark the landing deck on the floor.)
B is the pilot of the plane.
Together they work out some signals to communicate with each other. Some of the meanings might be —
'Too low. Go round again.'
'Plane on deck. Don't land.'
'Strong cross-winds. Take care.' 'All clear. Land immediately.'
Partners may want to work out other signals as well.
A then directs B with these signals.

10 Children relax on the ground outside, and look at the clouds floating overhead.
Are there clouds of different types?
Can clouds show us what the weather is going to be like?
Are there many differently shaped clouds? Some of these might remind you of different things.
Talk to someone near you about what you are seeing.

FLIGHT

TOUCHING ACTIVITIES

11 You are assembling a model plane from instructions that came in the box.

Can you work out what to do? How do you fix the different parts together? What type of aeroplane is it? Have you ever done this sort of thing before?

Some of the instructions are a bit complicated. How do you get on?

12 Activities with a balloon

Blow up the balloon and hold it by the neck. What do you think will happen if you let it go? Find out.

Blow it up again. This time, before you let it go, try to predict the flight path. Were you correct?

13 Blow up the balloon and tie a knot in the neck. How high can you hit it? Does it come straight down?

This time, hit it with another part of your body. Is that more difficult?

Lie on your back. Try to keep your balloon in the air by just using your feet and legs. Can you make it spin? Does it always come straight down?

See how much breath you need to keep the balloon up. What is the best way of blowing?

14 Make as many noises as you can with your balloon. What about humming against it, scraping it, rubbing it etc.

15 Lie on your stomach and put the balloon in front of your nose on the floor.

Try to nudge it along the floor by using your nose. After practising this, the children might enjoy a 'Balloon Race' where they can only use their noses to move their balloon.

16 With a partner

Partners stand facing each other holding the balloon between their stomachs. Without touching it with their hands, they find out if they can —

• Work it up to their chins.
• Turn around so that they are back to back without dropping the balloon.
• Sit down while still holding it between their backs.
• Get up again, still without dropping the balloon.
• Move around the room with the balloon held between stomachs or backs.

17 With a partner

Partners hit, pat, blow or kick the balloon to each other. They must not let it touch the floor.

18 Keep the Balloon Alive!

Groups of ten to twelve in a circle with five balloons.

People who have a balloon pat it to anyone in the circle. The person who gets it has to immediately pat it to someone else. Everyone has to keep their feet firmly planted on the floor, so leaping or moving to get the balloon is not allowed.

If a balloon lands on the floor out of reach, it is 'dead', and out of the game.

The game continues until all the balloons are 'dead'.

19 Balloon Kick

Groups of six with one balloon.

Each group sits in a circle, with legs stretched out in front and feet in the centre.

A balloon is tossed into the centre, and the group has to try to keep it in the air using only their feet.

If the balloon goes outside the circle, that group is 'out'.

The group that keeps the balloon in the air longest, is the winner.

TASTING AND SMELLING ACTIVITIES

20 You are an astronaut in a space capsule on your way to the moon. You have special high-energy food which is packed so that it won't leak in the weightless conditions.

What is the food and how is it packed?

You open the containers and taste it. Do you like it?

Tell someone near you how your food tastes and what it is.

21 You are an airport worker stacking containers of pre-cooked meals on to the plane.

Is it hot food, such as a casserole, or is it cold food like sandwiches and biscuits?

Handling all this food is making you very hungry, so you decide to sneak some while the supervisor is not looking.

You open one of the meals. What is it? You have to eat it quickly. How does it taste?

22 With a partner

Two chefs are planning the menus for a number of international airlines. The passengers are to have food that is traditional for the country to which they are flying.

What would be suitable menus for planes going to Greece, Italy, China, America, England, Spain? Try to work out a three course meal for these flights. Why not write and design your own menu?

FLIGHT

EXPLORING MOVEMENT AND SOUND
(INDIVIDUAL ACTIVITIES)

23 You are a bird hatching out of a shell.
Push with your feet, and your back, and your head.
Perhaps you can use your sharp beak to make a tiny hole. Try hard!
Now you have made the hole, it is easier to break out. One last big push — and you've made it!
How does the world look?
You are tired after your effort, so rest and relax.

24 You are a hawk flying way up in the sky.
You glide on air currents, and are lifted up and down as the breeze changes. The wind ruffles through your outstretched wings.
You are so high that you can see for miles.
Tell another hawk what you can see spread out below you.

25 The passenger plane is flying through a storm, which is tossing it around.
The hostess is trying to serve a meal. How does the rough weather affect her work? What happens when the plane hits an air pocket?

26 A kite competition
You are making your kite.
What material is it made of?
How is it constructed?
What type of kite is it?
Do you decorate it?
It is finished now, and all the kites are going to be flown. How do you get yours off the ground? It is a good windy day, so the kite soars into the air, and tugs at the string. How do you control it?

27 You are a stockman in the outback, rounding up cattle with a helicopter.
It is a big herd and difficult to keep moving, so you make the helicopter keep swooping and changing direction.

28 You are hang-gliding off a cliff at the ocean. There is a strong updraught which will help you get off the ground, but be careful as this can be very tricky.
How do you control the direction of your hang-glider? Can you do turns and glides in different directions?
It is very peaceful hanging above the sea as you watch the slow waves roll in to shore.

29 You are assembling your hang-glider on a cliff top.
How big is it? What is its shape and colour?
Spread it on the ground, and fix the struts in position. How do you attach these to the glider?
You will need to make sure your harness is securely fixed to the framework.
Check that everything is all right before you pick it up. Is it heavy? It is rather large and difficult to manage.

30 You are the fluffy thistle heads fully open, and ready to fly. A light breeze is blowing, and the seeds tremble on their stalks.
Suddenly, there is a strong puff of wind, and the thistle heads are blown away, spinning and flying in all directions. Where do they land?

EXPLORING MOVEMENT AND SOUND
(PARTNER Activities)

31 It is a hot, still, day in the bush. Although there are no animals or humans about, it is still a busy scene as dozens of insects hurry about their business.
What are they doing? Each insect makes a different sound as it flits around, and all of the sounds combine to form an insect chorus.

32 You have been to a fun-park where you bought an enormous balloon. You are now walking home with it.
The balloon is filled with hydrogen gas which is lighter than air, so the string is taut, and you have to keep a good grip on it to prevent the balloon from escaping. What colour is your balloon?
You open the front door, and manage to squeeze yourself and the balloon inside. Now, what will you tie the string to?
As you are doing this, it slips out of your grasp, and the balloon shoots up to the ceiling. The end of the string is well above your head. Can you get the balloon down?

33 A is a battery operated model plane. He is made of polystyrene foam, and has a rechargeable battery in his belly. B is flying the plane.
There is a gentle breeze blowing, and conditions are ideal for flying.
A crouches on the ground, while B connects the battery terminals to him and charges the battery. How long does it have to charge?
When everything is ready, B launches the plane. Does he face it into the breeze?
How does he get it off the ground?
Does B have any control of the plane in the air? Perhaps he has a remote control box.
What happens when A takes off? Perhaps the angle of flight is too steep, and the plane stalls and nosedives into the ground.
Perhaps it is a perfect flight, and the plane soars up, curves around, and lands next to B.
What sound does the plane make as it flies?
After the flight, the battery has to be recharged before the plane can take off again.

34 A is a specially shaped balloon without any air in him. He is flat and limp.
B is going to blow up A to discover what shape he is. Does B use his breath, or does he have a pump?
As B starts to blow, A grows and takes shape. What is the shape?
When A is fully blown up, B ties a string around the opening, and takes his big balloon for a walk.

35 Sky Diving

You are two professional sky divers in a light plane which is heading for the drop zone.

Check each other's harness to make sure your parachutes are securely strapped on. Ten seconds to go before you leave the plane. Are you ready?

You can see the target area far below.

GO!

36 You are two meteorology experts who are preparing to release a weather balloon.

The aluminium instrument box containing all your weather instruments has to be fastened under the balloon.

The balloon is to be filled with helium gas and you have a cylinder of the gas with you.

One of you is going to time the speed of the balloon's ascent and watch its direction.

When everything is ready, let the balloon go.

37 Two astronauts are strapped into their seats in the space capsule. The rocket is on the launching pad, about to take off on its journey to another planet.

The astronauts make sure that they are firmly strapped in, and check with Mission Control that everything is working correctly.

Now the countdown starts. (Teacher could now do the countdown from ten to zero.)

BLAST OFF!

38 Two astronauts are in the space capsule flying through outer space.

Because they are weightless, they can only move slowly and carefully to do the necessary tasks. What are they doing? They have to help each other with some jobs.

Some funny things can happen when you are weightless. Does anything funny happen to them?

FLIGHT

EXPLORING MOVEMENT AND SOUND
(GROUP ACTIVITIES)

39 Mother duck is taking her ducklings to the river. How do they move? Do they use their wings to keep their balance? Do they make any sounds as they waddle along?

When they reach the river they dive in for a swim. Do the ducklings know how to swim, or does the mother duck have to teach them?

40 A group of seagulls at the beach are scavenging food thrown by picnickers. They fight for the tastiest scraps, screeching and threatening each other. One gull snatches up a crust and flies off, with some of the others chasing him.

41 A swarm of bees are in their hive. Each bee has a different task to do, so all are humming about very busily.

What are they doing? They might be attending to larvae, mending or building the comb, storing pollen.

Just then, one bee who has been away from the hive returns with news of a paddock of flowers in full bloom. The bees become excited as they prepare to leave the hive. They all fly off to collect some pollen.

42 An aerobatic flying team is practising formation flying for an air pageant. They go through all their stunts, some of which are very difficult and thrilling.

43 A group of silly clowns are preparing to launch a home-made rocket. They hope to send a mouse into outer space!

The rocket has a long fuse which they will light when everything is ready. The clowns keep making funny mistakes and getting tangled up with each other. Finally they are ready to launch the rocket. Who lights the fuse? Do they take cover? What happens?

TALKING ACTIVITIES
(PARTNER AND GROUP)

44 Partners

A is the pilot of a commercial aircraft coming in to land at the airport.

B is the air traffic controller in the control tower.

B tells A which runway to use, the wind speed on the tarmac, and any other landing instructions.

A checks these, and prepares to land.

45 Partners

A new airline company is starting business. The Managing Director wants the uniforms of the hostesses to be smart and serviceable, but not to go out of style too quickly.

The two of you are to design these uniforms.

It would be an advantage if the fabric is washable and crease-resistant.

Do you think it is necessary to have a summer and a winter uniform?

Decide about the fabric, colour and style.

Perhaps it would help to make sketches as you go along.

46 Partners

Design a hot air balloon.

Does it carry passengers? How does it get the hot air supply? What is the balloon made of? What shape is most suitable? What is it designed to do? Is it for long or short flights? Will this make a difference to the design? How will the balloon return to the ground?

The partners will sketch and label their design.

47 Groups of ten to twelve

An historic hot air balloon flight is about to take place. The group is assembled around the huge balloon in a paddock. Those present include the two people making the flight; some relatives of theirs who have come to see them off; three workers who are loading and inflating the balloon, and will assist in the take off; some T.V. cameramen and journalists.

The workers prepare the balloon. What do the other people do? Perhaps the journalists want an interview.

48 Groups of six to eight

It is during a war, and the pilots on the aircraft carrier are relaxing.

What are they doing? They might be reading, eating, resting, playing cards, talking about home.

Suddenly, the general alarm is sounded. (Cymbal crash or drum roll.)

Action, as the pilots jump up, snatch their flying gear, and race to their planes.

49 Groups of four

On an aeroplane during a flight.

The hostess has problems with some passengers.

One is on his first flight, and is very nervous.

One is very demanding. He keeps asking for different things.

One is feeling airsick.

What can the hostess do to help them all?

50 Groups of ten to twelve

Three hijackers, passengers and crew.

Everything is normal on the passenger plane on an overseas flight.

FLIGHT

The hostesses are serving meals, the passengers are reading, eating, chatting etc.

Suddenly, three people stand up and reveal themselves as hijackers. What do they do? Are they armed? What are their demands? How do they try to get the plane to change course? Are they successful? What happens to the passengers?

(The three hijackers should get together first to plan their strategy, away from the rest of the group. This will add surprise to the actual hijack.)

Situations at an airport have lots of potential for partner and group discussions.

51 Groups of three

A is the daughter who is going overseas for a trip. B and C are her parents who are seeing her off.

Are the parents concerned for their daughter's safety on her trip? What sort of problems might they warn her about? Perhaps losing her money, the dangers of hitch-hiking, finding suitable accommodation, meeting people.

Does the daughter think all their warnings are necessary? Is she pleased that they are concerned for her, or does she get annoyed?

52 Groups of four or five

Grandma is going back to Greece for a visit. When the departure of her flight is announced, she doesn't want to leave. What does the family do? Do they try to persuade her to go? What sort of arguments might they use?

How does Grandma react to these arguments? What does she decide to do?

53 Groups of three or four

Two airport police at the passport check-out suspect a passenger of having a false passport. They think that he might be a criminal trying to leave the country illegally. They do not want to arouse his suspicions by arresting him outright, but they want to delay him, until headquarters can check his identity.

What delaying tactics do they use?

Does the passenger get suspicious?

How does it end up?

54 Partners

A passenger's baggage is missing from an overseas flight. He goes to the enquiry counter to try to find it.

What sort of description of the missing cases does he have to give the clerk?

Does he have to prove that the cases belong to him?

Does the clerk ask for any identification?

Is the passenger's baggage there or not?

55 Partners

During a routine customs inspection, the customs officer finds some illegal goods in a passenger's baggage.

What are the goods?

Does the passenger admit his guilt, or does he deny the bag is his?

What does the customs officer do?

What happens to the goods?

What happens to the passenger?

THINGS TO MAKE AND DO

Make some kites of different shapes. Which shape is the most efficient in flight? Why?

Make paper darts and have competitions to discover which one flies the furthest.

Play with Frisbees. How accurately can you hit a target?

Throw real boomerangs, or try to make one that will fly.

Make a parachute out of some fabric. Drop it from a height, and see what happens.

What do these mean —
Birds of a feather flock together.
A bird in the hand is worth two in the bush.
There's a good looking bird.
Breaking the sound barrier.

Observe cloud patterns during a day. Can you find the names for the different cloud formations? Can clouds help you predict the weather?

Make a graph or picture story to show cloud formations during a week.

Make a model of an airport.

Collect photos and pictures of aeroplanes.

Ask air travel agencies for brochures and posters of different airlines. You could visit them or write.

Assemble a model aeroplane from a kit.

Build an aeroplane out of large building blocks.

Use a balloon to make —
A face blow up balloon, texta-color the features, stick paper or wool on for the hair.
Piggy banks blow up a round balloon. Glue on lots of strips of newspaper. When hard and dry, cut the slot and decorate the pig.
Masks blow up a round balloon. Glue on lots of strips of newspaper. When hard and dry, carefully cut in half with a sharp knife. This makes two masks. Make holes at the side for tape or string. Decorate the face.

Do some bird-watching
Which birds visit the school ground? Can you discover their correct names? Which birds are native to Australia and which birds are not?
Tape bird calls. Play the tape to other people, and see if they can identify the birds.
Find out which trees the different birds like to perch in.
Set up a bird table in the school ground. Experiment to discover which food attracts most birds.
Obtain a chart of birds from the Gould League (State School No. 167, High Street, Prahran, Vic. 3181).
Identify the birds around your neighbourhood.
Collect different types of bird feathers. Can you identify them? Can you classify them?
Discover how birds build their nests. What time of year do they build them? Do different birds build different nests?

FLIGHT

READERS

Young Australia Language Development Scheme
Nelson   Reader No. 19

Macdonald First Library   1 book
Macdonald

Open Gate   2 books
Oliver & Boyd

Dolphin   4 books
University of London Press

Dolphin Science   6 books
University of London Press

Reason Why   3 books
Dobson

Action Books   1 book
Brockhampton

We Read About   3 books
Heinemann

Junior True Books   2 books
Muller

They Were First   1 book
Oliver & Boyd

The What Is It   4 books
Collins

Webster Series   1 book
Webster

True Adventure   1 book
Blackie

Adventures in Space   12 books
Hart-Davis

Lively Readers   1 book
Nelson

PIONEERING DAYS

PIONEERING DAYS

LISTENING ACTIVITIES

1 Go outside.
Children sit on the ground, and close their eyes.
Listen carefully to every sound that you can hear.
Open your eyes, and talk to someone about the sounds.
Now close your eyes again. This time you are trying to listen only to natural sounds, e.g. birds, wind in trees, water, rustling grass.
You are an early settler in Australia or New Zealand. You might be a gold miner, a drover, an explorer. What do these sounds mean to you?
Talk to someone about them.

2 This activity is for outside or inside.
Find some natural objects, e.g. sticks, leaves, rocks, dirt, sand, gravel. Use these to make sounds. Can you make several different sounds with the same objects?
Example: two sticks can be shaken in one hand; scraped or rubbed together; tapped together.
Find a partner and decide A and B.
A closes his eyes.
B makes a sound with his object.
A has to keep his eyes closed, and try to identify what object was used, and how the sound was made.

3 With a partner
Outside in a large space, e.g. oval, park, playground.
A and B stand facing each other about five metres apart. They take turns to call out to each other using different types of calls. They might whistle or yell, shout or scream. As they call the partners walk backwards.
How far can they separate before they cannot hear each other?
Can some calls be heard over longer distances? Which calls could be heard most clearly?
'Coo-ee' is a bush call that has been used in Australia for two hundred years. Try 'Coo-ee', and see how much distance you can cover.

4 Outside or inside
The whole grade sits in a circle formation. Divide the circle into three parts, with approximately the same number of children in each part. Call them part 1, 2, 3. (Telling you this is a bit basic I know, but young children in particular can get lost unless they know what's happening.)
Group 1 are going to hum on a single note. (I suggest **you** (the teacher) pick the note the first time.)
Group 2 are going to use their hands to make a sound, e.g. clap, slap thighs, click fingers.
Group 3 are going to hit two objects together, e.g. two pencils, sticks, small rocks.
You (teacher) are going to conduct, count, and call in the different groups. Now you are ready to start.
The aim is to build up a three layered sound which will sound a bit like an Aboriginal chant.

Suggestions
(a) Group 1 solo for beat of 4. Add Group 2. Continue for beat of 4. Add Group 3.

(b) Start with Group 3, then add Groups 2 and 1. Varying the leading group will give you six possible combinations.

(c) Vary the pitch of Group 1's note. The lower the note, the more dreamlike and mysterious the whole effect will be.

(d) Try syncopation of the rhythm. Sketch out this chart, and hang it up.

```
         1 2 3 4
Group 1  ■ ■ ■ ■
Group 2  ■ ■ ■ □
Group 3  ■ □ □ ■
```

Groups make their sound when their square is coloured. On first 4 beats;
Group 1 hum the 4.
Group 2 clap on 2nd and 3rd beats only.
Group 3 tap on 1st and 4th beats only.
(e) Let the groups choose other ways to make the rhythmic sounds.

(f) Ask the children to suggest other variations.

An example:

```
  1 2 3 4
  ■ □ ■ □
  □ ■ □ ■
  □ □ ■ □
```

PIONEERING DAYS

LOOKING ACTIVITIES

5 Go outside into the playground or a park.
Look carefully at the trees, bushes and grass.
How many different shades of green can you find?
Show them to a friend.
Pick one shade of green to look for.
Compare differently shaped leaves that are the same shade of green?
Show someone what you have found.

6 Collect some natural things that are brown.
What have you found? Do you have dirt, stones, rocks, bark, dry grasses and leaves?
Work with a partner, and sort your collections by colour.
How many different shades of brown do you have?
What is the darkest brown?
What is the lightest?
Can you sort your collection another way; e.g. by texture, weight, size, shape?

7 **With a partner**
A has a handful of small stones. He arranges them in a pattern or design on the floor, desk lid or table top while B watches. A must use all his stones.
As he does this, he talks to B about what he is doing.
A might arrange his stones to represent the sun, trees or animals, or he might just make a pattern that he likes.
When A has finished, B could guess what he has made, or comment on the pattern.

Then B has a turn.
(This activity could be tied in with Aboriginal art designs. Children may wish to find pictures or photos of these designs.)

8 **With a partner**
Trail blazing is a method by which explorers mark their path or trail so that they can find their way back home. With your partner work out —
• What your mark will be, e.g. arrow on the ground; crumpled ball of paper; broken stick; mark on a tree, desk or chair.
• Where your trail will go, e.g. across the room; around the schoolground; from your room, down the passage to another room.
Decide who is A and who is B.
A is going to blaze the trail, and B is going to try and follow it.
B does something else, such as read a book, talk to someone, play a game, while A blazes the trail.
A uses the method agreed on, to mark his path.
A must return for B within six minutes. Then both partners go over the trail together.
B tries to follow it, and A gives help, but only if B gets hopelessly confused.
When the children return, all could talk about the methods they used, and whether their partner managed to follow the trail.

9 Have a large sheet of paper prepared with dots and crosses scattered on it. This should be a secret from the children.

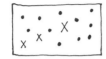

You are an early pioneer who owns a small flock of sheep. In the night, you heard a dingo in the paddock. You managed to scare it away by firing at it with your shotgun, but it was too dark to see if any sheep were killed.

It is now dawn, and you want to quickly check if all your sheep are all right.

I'm going to show you your paddock for five seconds. The dots are the live sheep, and the crosses are the ones that have been killed by the dingo.

(Now display your prepared paper and count to five. Cover it again and let the children talk freely about what they saw.)

If they get stuck, you could direct their thoughts with such questions as —

How many sheep were killed?

How many are all right?

How many are in your whole flock, both dead and alive?

Were you able to count them all?

How did you do this?

Variations

Make up a story about other animals; horses, cattle, hens, ducks, pigs. Change the attacker.

Add or subtract to the dots and crosses on the paper. The older the children, the more marks they will be able to cope with.

PIONEERING DAYS

TOUCHING ACTIVITIES

10 Try and find some things in the room that are made of wood.
What have you found?
Close your eyes and feel some of these things.
Can you describe how they feel?
They might be rough, smooth, splintery, knobbly, bumpy, scratchy, prickly.
Look at your wood very carefully.
Can you see the grain in it?
Can you feel the grain?
How does it feel?
Are there any other marks or holes in the wood?
Tell someone near you what you are discovering.

11 Go for a walk around your school. Find some things that have an interesting texture.
How do tree trunks feel?
What about smooth twigs and logs?
Can you find any other smooth-feeling growing things?
You might find something that is dry and crackly.
How does this feel?
Try feeling these things with many different parts of your body. You could rub them against your cheek and your forehead and your back.
You could stroke them with your elbow, tap them with the back of your hand and your knee, squeeze and pinch them with your fingers.
Talk to a friend about what you can feel as you are doing this.

12 You are a trooper carefully grooming your horse.
The governor of the colony is going to inspect your regiment today, and you want your horse to look his best.
What is your horse's name?
What do you use to groom him?
He is sixteen hands high, so you have to stand on tiptoe to comb and brush his back.
Try and get your horse's coat silky smooth and shiny. You may have to brush rather hard.
Some burrs and prickles are tangled in its mane and tail. How will you get these out?
Be careful not to prick your fingers!
Perhaps you should inspect your horse's feet to make sure there are no stones stuck under its shoes.
It's almost time for the inspection parade, so finish quickly.

13 You are a pioneer settler making mud bricks for your hut.
You have a big pile of mud, a pile of sand, some straw and some water in an old tin.
How much sand do you add to the mud?
Do you have a shovel to use, or not? Mix it up well.
Do you need to add much water, or is the mixture already pretty sloppy?
What do you do with the straw?
Do you have a wooden mould to shape the bricks, or do you shape them by hand?
The mud is heavy and sticky and clings to your fingers. How does it feel?
When you have made your bricks, set them to dry in the sun. Now you had better clean yourself up.

14 With a partner

A is a huge gold nugget. It is almost completely buried in rock and dirt, except for a tiny corner which is above the ground.

B is a prospector on the goldfields. For weeks he has been searching for gold, and now he can see the shiny edge of the big nugget. He starts to carefully scrape the dirt away from the nugget. He feels very excited as more and more gold starts to show.

It looks like the biggest nugget in the world!
Does B work quickly because he is excited, or slowly because he doesn't want to damage the nugget?
When B has uncovered A how does he feel?
He examines it very carefully, and brushes off any loose dirt.
B might want to show his find to another gold prospector.

PIONEERING DAYS

TASTING AND SMELLING ACTIVITIES

15 Go outside. Find some leaves, rocks or earth that have a pleasant or unpleasant smell.
Is it a strong smell, or a faint one?
Can you find two different things that smell like each other?
Does what you have found look like it would smell good or bad?
Can you find any rotting things? (Wood, fungus, leaves, fruit.)
How do they smell? Can you describe the smell?
Talk to a friend about it.

16 Outside with a partner
A closes his eyes.
B leads him to some natural things that smell interesting, e.g. leaves, berries, flowers, rocks, dirt.
A keeps his eyes closed, and smells them. Can he work out what they are?
Do leaves have a stronger smell when they are crunched up?
Perhaps B might try this out.

17 You are an escaped convict who has spent two days and nights hiding in the bush. You haven't had anything to eat since you escaped, so you are starving.
This morning you managed to trap a goanna which you are going to cook.
Are you going to skin it, or hope the skin burns off as it cooks?
Are you going to try and hang it above the flames in some way, or just throw it on the fire?
You are so hungry that you can't wait too long.

How does it smell as it sizzles in the flames?
Perhaps it is ready to eat. You are not sure because you have never cooked a goanna before!
It doesn't look too good, but you don't have any other food. See how it tastes.
Are you going to eat it?

18 With a partner
The new governor of the colony is giving his first dinner party. He has spoken to you both, his two cooks, about how he wants to impress his guests with very special food for the occasion.
All you have is fish that is already two days old, and some mutton.
The fish looks dull and limp. How does it smell?
Will you bake, fry or grill it?
What can you add to make it taste all right?
While the fish is cooking, you prepare the mutton.
Is the mutton fresh, or has it been hanging around for a few days as well?
Maybe if you add lots of onions and herbs it might improve the taste. Does it? What else could you add?
How is the fish going? Does it smell any better? How does it taste now?
When everything is cooked, you arrange it attractively on the big serving dishes.
What might the guests say about your special meal?

19 With a partner
You are the children of a pioneer family who live in a small settlement. Your mother has sent you

both to pick blackberries, as she is going to make blackberry pie for dinner.

The berries are large and juicy, and just ready to eat. Do you have a billy or bucket to put them in? Try not to squash the ripe blackberries as you pick them.

Every now and then you eat some as you work. How do they taste?

Be careful not to get blackberry juice on your clothes, because it stains.

The bushes are very prickly, and some of the berries are hard to reach. That looks a nice one.

How does it taste?

Keep picking, and see if you can fill your bucket.

PIONEERING DAYS

EXPLORING MOVEMENT AND SOUND
(INDIVIDUAL ACTIVITIES)

20 You are an early settler clearing trees off your land.

Before you start cutting trees, you will need to sharpen your axe.

What do you use to sharpen it?

How do you keep your axe steady while you are sharpening it?

The edge looks about ready now. Can you test it somehow, to see if it is really sharp?

Now you can start chopping down the trees. Get a good grip on the axe. (Supply a steady beat for the chopping. Tap tambourine, hand drum, thump a table, stamp your foot.)

It's hard work, but you are strong.

You are nearly through. Be careful of the falling tree!

What sounds does the tree made as it crashes?

21 The only place to wash your clothes on the gold-fields is in the creek.

What do you have to wash? (Shirt, pants, skirt, dress, socks.)

You have a bar of soap which you made yourself, and it doesn't lather up very well. Your clothes are full of dust from the gold diggings, and you have to scrub really hard to get them clean.

You might beat them on the flat rocks, to get out some of the dust.

22 You are an Aboriginal hunter fishing with a spear in a deep still river pool. You might be standing on the river bank, or balanced on a smooth rock in the middle.

You must keep perfectly still, and just watch the water for any ripples or bubbles that will let you know a fish is there.

Can you see any dark shapes moving through the still water?

That looks like a fish.

Do you have your spear balanced and ready to throw?

Drive it in hard!

Did you get the fish?

23 You are a goanna sunning itself on a smooth rock. It is peaceful and quiet in the bush, and you feel very sleepy and comfortable. You can hear tiny insects buzzing around, and far in the distance there is the sound of running water.

One insect lands gently on your foot. It feels tickly, but you are too sleepy to move. If you wiggle just your toes it might fly off. There it goes.

It is so warm and comfortable on this big smooth rock. Have a big slow stretch and a big yawn.

24 You are a sheep shearer in the early days in Australia or New Zealand. You use hand clippers to shear the sheep. These look a bit like scissors with wide blades.

(Can you find a picture of them for the children?)

You are the ringer in the shed — the top shearer — so you are really expert at this shearing game.

Before you start, check your clippers to make sure they are working smoothly.

Drag out a sheep and get it into position for shearing.

How do you hold the sheep so that it doesn't struggle?

Which part of the sheep do you start on?

You try to cut as close to the sheep's skin as possible.

What happens if your shears slip, and you cut the sheep's skin?

When you finish shearing that sheep, you start on the next.

25 You are one of a group of explorers in the early days of Australia or New Zealand. You left camp before the others woke up to search for food, but you have had an accident.

You might have fallen off a cliff, stumbled into a swamp, been knocked by a falling tree, or fallen into a pit.

You have been injured in some way, and find you cannot move.

What has happened to you?

Have you broken a leg or an arm?

Are you pinned down by a rock or tree?

If so, what part of your body is caught?

You also find that you cannot speak, but you can make sounds.

Can you make these sounds loudly enough for the other explorers to hear?

(Give the children time to experiment with this.)

You hear the others coming, so keep making sounds to tell them where you are.

(More time for sounds.)

You are on very dangerous ground. Try to warn them with your sounds.

(Sounds will now take on a different quality.)

Now they can see you. Let them know what your problem is.

26 It is the middle of the long, dry summer in the outback. For days a hot, dusty north wind has been blowing, and the trees and grass are tinder dry. It's real bushfire weather.

You are camping out under a tree, and boiling the billy over your small camp fire. Suddenly, a spark leaps out of the fire, lands on some dry grass, and starts to burn.

What can you do?

The fire starts to spread!

(Shake the tambourine to give the sound of the crackling fire.)

Flames are licking at the base of the tree. You've got to put it out. Once the fire reaches the branches there's no way of stopping it!

Perhaps you can stamp out the flames, or beat them out with your jacket or a branch that you frantically tear off a small tree.

(Increase pace of tambourine sound, then gradually fade it away.)

What happened?

Did you manage to put the fire out?

27 You are a convict who has escaped into the bush. As you fled, you were able to grab a small axe. This helps you hack your way through the thick undergrowth, but your bare arms and legs are still getting scratched by thorns, and your clothes ripped by sharp branches and twigs.

PIONEERING DAYS

Stop and listen for a moment. What's that sound?
It might be the troopers and their dogs after you.
You've got to hurry, but the bush is so thick.
You're hot and sweating and scratched and bruised and stung by insects.
And you're scared!

EXPLORING MOVEMENT AND SOUND
(PARTNER ACTIVITIES)

28 Two bushrangers are being hunted by troopers. They are on foot, as their horses were shot from under them.
In that attack, one bushranger has been wounded in the leg.
It is rough country and they are trying to move as quickly as they can.

29 Two explorers are climbing a dangerous cliff.
They are both wearing a heavy pack of supplies which weighs them down.
What is in the packs?
Is there anything dangling from the outside, such as a rope or billy?
It is hard and dangerous work, and they need to rest often.
After a rest, they decide to rope themselves together for safety.
How does this make them safer?
Where do they tie the rope?
They take turns to lead as they struggle up the cliff face.

30 You are two explorers who are trying to cross a flooded river. It is really swollen, and a strong current is flowing. You watch whole trees being carried downstream in the raging water, and you realise that this is going to be a very dangerous crossing.
What else can you learn from watching the river?
You might be able to use some of your explorer's equipment to help you cross, such as a stout rope or an axe.

You have to get across, so make a plan about how you'll do it.
(Give the children time to talk and argue about this. Two minutes is enough.)
What is on the opposite bank?
Are there trees and rocks, or is it a steep bank going straight down?
You've seen trees being pushed downstream, so you know the water will be above your head.
How are you going to get your equipment and stores across?
(Give the children a few more minutes to plan these extra ideas.)
Now you are ready to go. Good luck and take care.

31 A and B are gold prospectors who are panning for gold in a river.
How big are your pans?
How do you scoop up the gravel and wash it?
Are you finding any specks of gold?
You are friends who are working together, so you talk and show each other what you are finding.
Suddenly, A notices that he has washed a whole pan full of small gold nuggets! What does he do?
Does he tell B, or try to keep it a secret?
What happens?

32 You and your pioneer friend have built your hut near a small creek. Normally the level of the water is well below the bank, but for the last few days you have noticed that the water has been running faster than usual, and closer to the top. It has also changed from being clear to a murky brown.
What might be causing all this? Somewhere upstream, more water must be coming in to the creek.
You could be in for a flood.
How are you going to protect your property from the flood?
Can you build up the river bank with big rocks?
Perhaps you could chop down some saplings, and use them to strengthen the bank.
What else could you use?
Everything is really heavy, so you need to help each other.

33 You are two pioneer settlers building a fence to stop your horses from wandering away.
While one settler cuts and trims some suitable trees for the fence posts, the other settler digs the post holes. The holes have to be deep enough to hold the posts securely. The ground is hard and flinty, so you might have to break up the surface with a pick.
Logs for the posts have to be cut to the same length so the fence will look even. How will you make sure of this?
When the holes and the logs are ready, start erecting your fence.

34 A and B are two Aboriginals preparing for a corroboree. They are going to decorate each other's bodies for the occasion. They might paint on different designs which mean special things to them.

PIONEERING DAYS

Crushed up rocks and earth mixed with water make the paint, and pliable twigs are the brushes.

They have some soft birds' feathers to stick in a pattern on their skin. What can they use to stick them on? Perhaps sticky sap is in the stems of some fleshy plants.

Can you make an interesting design on each other's backs?

When the Aboriginals are ready, they practise their dancing for the corroboree. (Supply a slow steady beat for the children to move to.)

35 A is a primitive Aboriginal artist painting a picture on a rock wall. He wants to paint various aspects of Aboriginal life such as hunting, dancing, searching for food, making a fire.

Can you think of any other things that he should paint?

B is the artist's model, so he poses in different ways that show some of the daily tasks. He might freeze in a spear-throwing position, or pose as if he is digging up leaves and berries for food.

Does A tell B how to stand, or does he leave the choice to B?

A quickly paints his picture on the wall, then B changes to another pose.

What does A use for paint and brushes?

Does he make big paintings or small ones?

In what order does A paint these scenes on the wall?

EXPLORING MOVEMENT AND SOUND
(GROUP ACTIVITIES)

36 In a hall, general purpose room, or outside.
(Divide the grade into three equal groups.)
You are local farmers on a kangaroo drive. You want to chase away a mob of kangaroos that have been eating the grass, and breaking down your paddock fences. You are going to scare the kangaroos, by making a lot of noise as you walk towards the creek.
(Teacher should locate the creek in one area of the room or playground. It helps smooth the organisation.)
So the kangaroos don't slip past us, we are going to spread out in three long lines at the edges of the paddock, and approach the creek from three different directions.
Remember to make lots of noise.
Stop when you reach the creek.

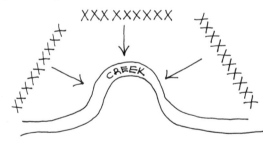

(Make sure all the children are in position before you give the signal to start.)
When the children reach the 'creek', let them sit down and talk about the noises they made, the way they moved, and how many kangaroos were driven away.

Variation
Two groups are farmers.
One group is the kangaroos. They should decide where they are in the paddock; what they are doing (feeding, lying down etc.); how they will cross the creek.

37 Groups of five or six
A posse of troopers and two Aboriginal trackers are out searching for a notorious gang of bushrangers. Neither Aboriginal can speak English, so they have to communicate with the troopers in sign language and sounds.
As the Aboriginals search the ground, they talk to each other in their own language.
What are they looking for?
How can they communicate this to the troopers?
How can they communicate this sort of information to the troopers?
After a while, the Aboriginals realise that they are getting close to the bushrangers' hideout.
How do they inform the troopers?
What plans do the troopers make?
Will they attack or ambush?

38 Groups of six to eight
A convict gang is building a road through the bush.
It is a very hot still day, and they have been working for hours in the blazing sun.
Are the convicts chained together?
What tools do they have to work with? Are these tools heavy?

PIONEERING DAYS

What is the country like?
Are rocks and logs in the way of the new road?
How do they clear them away?
Perhaps flies and biting insects annoy the convicts.

39 Groups of five or six
A party of explorers are slowly working their way up the side of a mountain. They have reached a narrow ledge, with a great wall of rock on one side, and a sheer drop on the other.
Do they have pack horses with them? If so, how are the horses reacting to this climb?
What can the explorers do to try and soothe the horses?
As they round a corner, they find an obstacle in their path.
What is it? How do they solve this problem?

40 Groups of five or six
A family of settlers is building a hut in the bush.
They have selected the best place to put the hut, and are now clearing the land and cutting trees for the framework.
Do they use axes or crosscut saws?
They don't have any nails, so how will they fasten the logs together?
What will they use for the walls?
How can they attach the walls to the frame without any nails?
What about the roof?
There might be some big leafy branches around that would make good cover.

The dirt floor will have to be tramped down hard to get it even and flat.
It is hard and tiring work, and sometimes they stop and rest.

41 Groups of five to eight
On the goldfields, a group of hopeful gold prospectors are sinking a mine shaft. This is the second day of their work, so they have already dug a fairly deep hole. Some miners dig with picks and shovels, some haul up the dirt and pile it near the mouth of the shaft.
The ground is dry and crumbly, so the walls of the shaft might have to be reinforced with saplings.
Who will cut and trim these, and get them ready to use?
As they work, the miners all keep looking for signs of gold.

TALKING ACTIVITIES
(PARTNER)

42 A is a storekeeper in the town.

B is a customer who is buying supplies for a journey to the goldfields.

Work out together what the customer will need for his trip.

Are all the items needed in stock?

Are they expensive, or does the customer get some bargains?

Can the storekeeper make a bigger sale by persuading the customer to buy more than he needs?

43 A is a helpful and experienced goldminer.

B is a new chum who has just arrived on the goldfields.

A gives B advice on —
- How to dig or pan for gold.
- How to recognise gold when he finds it.
- What equipment he will need.
- A likely spot to start digging.

B questions A when necessary.

44 A and B discover that they have both pegged out a claim over the same ground.

Both try to prove that they have a legal right to the claim.

How do they do this?

Can they decide whose claim it is, or do they come to some compromise?

45 A and B are two pioneer women on the goldfields. Together they talk over the day-to-day problems of this way of life.

They might share their experiences of the hardships of —
- Keeping their tents or huts clean.
- Buying and cooking food.
- Caring for children and husbands.

Are they worried about bringing up their children on the goldfields?

How is this way of life different from their old life in Britain?

What are their hopes and fears for the future?

46 A is a trooper who has to inspect miners' licences to dig for gold.

Is he experienced in this work or not?

How does he feel about miners needing to have licences?

B is the gold miner who is being asked to show his licence.

Does he have one?

If he does, is it a current licence or out of date?

What is the punishment if he doesn't have a licence?

How does the miner feel about the trooper?

(This activity could follow discussion and research about the whole aspect of licences and relationships between the miners and the troopers. An actual licence which the children have drawn up would provide them with something concrete to work with.)

47 A is a dressmaker in the new colony.

B is the governor's wife who has come to order a dress for the forthcoming ball.

PIONEERING DAYS

Does the dressmaker have any new fabrics to show?

Of course the governor's wife wants to look elegant and up-to-date in fashion.

Can the dressmaker help her to choose a style for the dress?

Has the dressmaker made clothes for her before, or is this the first time?

Is the dressmaker a convict or a free settler? Will this affect the way the governor's wife speaks to her?

How much will the dress cost, and how long will it take to make?

They both should be happy with the final decision.

(Partners could sketch the final design.)

48 A is a government official who wants a new house.

B is an architect.

What are the official's needs in a house, e.g. number of rooms, entertainment areas, layout of grounds?

What building materials does the architect suggest, e.g. local stone, timber, convict-made brick?

Does he prefer one more than the others? What reasons can he give for this?

What does the proposed building site look like?

Is is flat, hilly, rocky?

Is it close to people or isolated?

Will this influence the design of the house?

(Partners could make some rough sketches.)

49 A is organising an exploration party.

Where does he plan to go?

B is very keen to join the group, but A thinks he will not be suitable, so he is trying to talk B out of going.

What sort of arguments will A use to deter B? He might emphasise the dangers of exploration.

What are these dangers?

The isolation and hardships which are part of exploring should be explained. Perhaps A might exaggerate these a bit.

Why is B so keen to go?

Can he persuade A by giving his reasons?

50 A is a member of a famous gang of bushrangers.

B is a young person who wants to join the gang.

What skills does B have that will be useful to the bushrangers?

Can he shoot accurately?

Does he have a good fast horse?

Does he know the country well?

Has he friends among the settlers who will be able to provide food and shelter when necessary?

How can he prove all this, and persuade A to let him join?

What questions will A want to ask B to make sure he is not a police spy?

What does A finally decide?

TALKING ACTIVITIES
(GROUP)

51 Groups of five to seven

Tonight is the governor's ball, the social event of the season.

The maids are bustling round, helping their mistresses to prepare.

Do the ladies have new gowns? What style, colour and fabric are they?

Are they pleased with their dresses, or do some ladies feel a bit discontented?

The maids help the ladies to style their hair, put on their dresses, and generally do as they are told.

What do the ladies talk about as they get dressed and ready?

How do they talk to their maids?

52 Groups of four or five

A family has decided to leave the town to try their luck on the goldfields.

Who are the family members? Are there old people as well as young ones?

Who decided that they would go? Does everyone in the family want to go?

What plans will they have to make before they can leave?

It will be a long and tiring journey, so they will have to make plans about food, water, shelter on the way, transport.

They are excited about their journey, but also a bit worried. What might they be worried about?

53 Groups of five or six

Two group members are explorers (or drovers) who are setting out in search of new land to settle.

The other group members are their families, e.g. wives, parents, brothers and sisters.

Where are the two going?

Will it be a hard journey?

How long do they think they will be away?

Do their families have any last minute instructions or warnings for them?

What will the families do while the two are on their journey?

Do their families want them to go, or not? Perhaps some members try to persuade them to stay.

What reasons do the two give for going? (Fame, money, land for themselves . . .)

54 Groups of five to eight

A gang of bushrangers are in their hideout. They have just returned from a successful raid on a gold bearing coach, and are dividing the loot amongst themselves.

There are bags of gold dust, and some money and jewellery which they stole from the passengers.

Who decides how it will be divided?

Does the head of the gang get more than the others?

Did they all play an equal part in the hold-up, or did some do more than others?

Are all the bushrangers happy about the division of loot?

Who has the final say on who gets what?

55 Groups of five or six

A group of desperate convicts are planning an escape from a penal settlement.

PIONEERING DAYS

Why do the convicts want to escape?

What is life like in their prison?

Have they all been there for the same number of years, or are some of them new arrivals?

Is there a leader of this gang? If so, how has he been chosen?

The convicts will need to consider many things if their escape is to be successful.

Examples —

Timing of the break-out.

The actual spot from which they will make their escape bid.

What the sentries will be doing at this time.

What equipment and food they can steal to help them survive in the bush.

Where they will head for after they break out, and if they'll stay together or split up into pairs.

They will need to choose who will do each task to prepare for the escape.

Who will get to know the sentries' routine?

Who will steal the food, and how?

Who will steal equipment, and what will it be?

The convicts may sketch out a rough plan of the settlement showing sentries' posts, possible escape routes, and anything else of importance.

(The children may draw on their knowledge of war escape films, which are pretty much the same situation. Encourage this, as it will help provide them with background reference material.)

56 Groups of five or six

Many Aboriginal legends tell the stories of how different things were created. There are stories about how the sun was formed, and how certain native animals became the way they are now.

These stories are often called legends of the Dreamtime, and were made up before the white man came to Australia.

In your group, try to make up a Dreamtime legend. The story is to explain how something changed to become the way it is now.

Some starter ideas —

How the desert was formed.

How Ayers Rock was formed.

How the echidna got his spikes.

Why the kangaroo hops.

Why the emu cannot fly.

After the children have made up their legends, they could tell them to other groups, record them on tape, write them down and illustrate them. These written stories could then be bound into a class book.

It would be interesting to find an authentic Dreamtime legend on the same topic. (There is one about the echidna.) Read legends to the children so that they could compare them.

THINGS TO MAKE AND DO

Make some natural dyes. Try onion skins, beetroot, crushed up chalk and coloured rocks.

Tie-dye a tee shirt or handkerchief.

Make jewellery using natural things like seeds and shells.

Try and get some raw wool, and process it.

Sing 'Click Go the Shears' and 'Waltzing Matilda'.

Find someone who can use a spinning wheel, and watch them spin.

Erect a tent in the school ground.

Build a campfire.

Have a barbecue lunch.

Find out what 'damper' is and how to make it.

Make bark and stone rubbings. Hold the paper against the bark, and rub over it with a thick crayon.

Make some paper.

Make some mud bricks.

Make some soap.

Listen to records of Aboriginal songs.

Read some Dreamtime legends.

Hold a 'Pioneering Days' day when everyone dresses up.

Draw up a gold miner's licence.

Try and find out how much a ball and chain weighed. Find something the same weight, and carry it around for a while. Now you know how the convicts felt!

Read these poems. 'The Fire at Ross' Farm' by Henry Lawson and 'The Man from Snowy River' by 'Banjo' Paterson.

Find out the names of some early Australian explorers, and what they did.

Make a list of places that are named after famous explorers or early settlers, e.g. Hume Highway, Port Macquarie, Arthur's Pass, Bank's Peninsula.

Find out about these people: Sir Peter Buck, Senator Bonner, Sir Douglas Nicholls, Albert Namatjira, Harold Blair, Evonne Goolagong, Sir Erua Tirikatini.

Turn your room into an early pioneering town. You could draw a plan of it.

Make a gold diggings in the corner of the playground. Dig for gold. You never know, you might find some.

PIONEERING DAYS

Go on an excursion to a gold mining town, an old convict prison, a pioneering museum.

Find out about —
Swagmen.
Why distant hills look blue.
'Bush Telegraph'.
Coolgardie safes.
Australian gemstones.
Orienteering.
Deer stalkers.

Identity is a quarterly magazine published by the Aboriginal Publications Foundation Inc. It is a good source of information on Aboriginals today. Why not take out a subscription ($6.00 inc. postage) by writing to Shop 9, International House, 2 Irwin Street, Perth 6000.

READERS

Young Australia Language Development Scheme Nelson	Readers No. 22, 23
Legends of the Aborigines Reed	12 books
Scholastic Core Ashtons	3 books
Young Puffins Penguin	13 books
Dolphin Science University of London	1 book
Trend Cheshire	25 books
Endeavour Jacaranda	3 books
Animals of Many Lands Chapman	1 book
Reading Systems Scott Foresman	Level 9
Gage World Community Study	1 book